NATO
Air-Launched
Weapons

Jeremy Flack

The Crowood Press

First published in 2002 by
The Crowood Press Ltd
Ramsbury, Marlborough
Wiltshire SN8 2HR

British Library Cataloguing-in-Publication Data
A catalogue record for this book is available from the British
Library.

ISBN 1 86126 501 8

All photographs by the author / API Photo Library unless
otherwise indicated.

Designed and typeset by:
Focus Publishing
11a St Botolph's Road,
Sevenoaks,
Kent TN13 3AJ

Printed and bound in Malaysia by Times Offset (M) sdn bhd

CONTENTS

Maritime Weapons

New Weapons

The development of air-launched weapons has seen advances every bit as staggering as those elsewhere in the 100-year history of aviation. Initially seen as a reconnaissance platform to replace balloons, early military aircraft were unarmed, although pilots often had a pistol in case they came down behind enemy lines. Opposing aircraft seldom met, but when they did it proved tempting to take pot shots at each other. Whilst flying over enemy lines, dropping a few hand grenades kept the enemy's heads down when observing their positions.

It was not long before these haphazard and primitive methods were improved upon. The pistols were replaced by machine guns and led to fighter aircraft. At the same time the grenade dropping led to the bomber aircraft, but the fragility and limited power of early aircraft limited the effectiveness of the these. Airships were also used to drop bombs, but again these were small and often incendiary for effect. By the end of World War One, however, bomb capacity had crept up with the Handley Page 0/100 capable of carrying sixteen 112lb (51kg) bombs.

World War Two saw the development of aircraft as a major war machine and the development of famous fighters such as the Spitfire, P-51 Mustang and Bf 109, but their armament was still based on the machine gun, although more sophisticated than before and including large-calibre cannon. Their success was dependent on performance and the pilot's capability in one-to-one combat.

Developments in bomber design led to ever greater bomb loads being carried. Towards the end of the war modified Lancaster bombers were able to carry the 22,000lb (10,000kg) Grand Slam bomb. Bombing techniques improved but still mostly involved 'carpet' bombing with large numbers of aircraft obliterating whole areas of cities: precision bombing was relatively difficult and so to ensure destruction of targets large numbers of bombers were mustered, leading to the '1,000-bomber' raids. These attacks also produced huge numbers of civilian casualties. For accurate precision bombing a different type of flying was required. One of the more famous was the attack by very low-flying RAF Mosquito bombers on the Amiens Gaol on 18 February 1944, when Gestapo records were destroyed in a building in which many French underground prisoners held on the upper storeys nonetheless survived the attack. World War Two ended with the dropping of the two atom bombs.

The Germans had experimented in using rockets to attack formations of Allied bombers during the war, but these were only built in small quantities. Developments in hand by the end of the war included wire guidance. Rockets were also used by both sides to attack ground targets from around the middle of the war: early RAF examples consisting merely of a solid fuel rocket powering a solid steel warhead proved effective against tanks and submarines. These were mostly unguided and depended on the skill of the pilot for their accuracy. However, a few radio-controlled flying bombs, of varying effectiveness, were developed, and even primitive television- and infrared-guided gliding bombs.

Advances in the 1950s led to a wide range of devastating weaponry such as air-to-air missiles armed with atomic warheads intended to explode in the middle of bomber formations, and a succession of atomic bomb-armed air-to-ground missiles. Fortunately none of these were ever used, but an ever increasing range of conventional air-launched weapons continued to be developed.

The unguided air-to-air rockets designed to shoot down enemy aircraft gave way to guided missiles. Initially, these missiles had a short range and their IR (infrared) heat-seeking guidance was of limited effectiveness: they could be easily distracted by the sun or even reflections off lakes. Missiles such as the radar-guided AIM-7 Sparrow and heat-seeking AIM-9 Sidewinder began their development during the later 1940s and entered service during the mid 1950s. The Russians produced what appeared to be a Sidewinder replica, which entered service in the early 1960s.

The Vietnam War saw the introduction of 'Wild Weasel' aircraft intended to protect aircraft formations against SAMs (surface-to-air missiles) with the Shrike anti-radiation missile. These reduced US aircraft loss rates from 5.7 per cent in 1965 to 1.75 per cent in 1967. While carpet bombing continued from B-52D bombers capable of carrying in the region of 60,000lb (27,000kg) of bombs, this conflict also saw the concentrated development of guided weapons culminating in the Paveway LGB (laser-guided bomb) during the mid-1960s.

The development of miniaturized electronic components in replace of the previous valve technology has led to the practical development of a broad range of air-launched weapons. Over the last forty years not only has their reliability and accuracy greatly improved, but their capabilities have been remarkably enhanced, most recently with the incorporation of GPS (Global Positioning System) navigation in both missiles and bombs.

For the first time in over fifty years of existence, the NATO inventory now includes Russian-built weapons. Following the end of the Cold War, former Warsaw Pact countries Hungary, Poland the Czech Republic and, through its reunification with West Germany, the former German Democratic Republic, have now joined NATO. A number of other countries are interested in joining and so additional air-launched weapons may be added to NATO's inventory in the future.

In compiling the entries for this book, it has not always been clear exactly which older weapons are still being held available for possible use. While many obsolete weapons have been destroyed, some have been sold or supplied to other countries within or outside NATO, and others may be retained in reserve even though they may be seldom seen on display. They may be occasionally seen on weapon-firing practice exercises where aircrew need to be kept current in their use. The high technology used in most modern weaponry comes at a price, and as a result few older weapons can be replaced on a one-for-one basis. Often the improved efficiency of such weapons means that they do not need to be used in the same numbers to achieve the same result.

Over the years each country has purchased weapons according to its perceived needs. The acquisition of a particular weapon as opposed to another does not always follow a military logic, as political considerations may be involved: the employment of the purchasing nation's workforce and/or foreign exchange may have a greater priority. As a result the composition of each NATO member's armoury contains many similar weapons designed for similar roles. Although numerous joint exercises have been held by NATO members over the years, such exercises can never wholly replicate real operations, and during the troubles in the Balkans these weapon differences caused a few problems. Some difficulties arose where capabilities of some equipments or weapons with a similar role did not match exactly, or required a slightly differing method of operation. While this is a problem and cannot be completely resolved, the use of offset agreements may be one partial solution: under such agreements, the country where a weapon is manufactured is required to purchase goods of a similar value from the country buying the weapon. In addition, the recent reduction in the number of manufacturers may help to improve the standardization of weapons.

I have divided this book into sections of air-to-air missiles, rockets, air-to-ground weapons and naval weapons. I have also included a section on new weapons that may be about to enter service with a NATO country, or are in development and will probably enter service with a NATO country. While I hope that the main sections are comprehensive, the last section is subjective to a degree and is included to show the range and capabilities that are likely to used in the future.

I have included some rocket-launcher pods, but these are representative and are not intended to be comprehensive. Russia and the former Warsaw Pact countries have a wide range of bombs and cluster bombs, and include some stocks of old weapons. This edition contains a representative selection and it is hoped that a future editions may be more comprehensive.

Should any readers be aware of any weapons that have been omitted from the main sections I would be interested to hear from them especially if they have photographic evidence. I can be contacted at: Aviation Photographs International, 15 Downs View Road, Swindon, Wiltshire, SN3 1NS, United Kingdom.

I would like to thank the various manufacturers who have supplied information and photographs. I would also like to thank Tech Sgt Langden as well as his team from the 49th OG who arranged for a range of USAF weapons to be made available for me to photograph.

I would also like to thank Wendy Buckle and the Cranfield University / Royal Military College of Science for their valuable assistance.

9M39 IGLA (SA-18 'GROUSE') MISSILE

Manufacturer:	Not known
Country of manufacture:	Russia
Diameter:	2.83in (72mm)
Span:	9.84in (250mm)
Length:	5.54ft (1.69m)
Weight:	24lb (10.8kg)

A pair of 9M39 missiles in the launcher. The spherical objects are nitrogen bottles which supply coolant for the IR seekers.

The 9M313 Igla is similar in size to the US Stinger missile and followed a similar development sequence. It too was originally designed as a surface-to-air missile in the mid 1970s and subsequently adapted for use as an air-to-air missile for helicopters.

The Igla has been built in two models. The 9M313 Igla 1 has been allocated the NATO reporting designation SA-16 'Gimlet' and the 9M39 has been allocated SA-18 'Grouse'. While little is known of the difference between the two missiles the launcher is distinctive from earlier sim-

ilar missiles with its conical protective nose cover.

The Igla has been fitted on the Ka-50, Mi-17, Mi-24 and Mi-28 and used by many operators of these types including the Czech, Hungarian and Polish armies.

AIM-7 SPARROW MISSILE

Manufacturer:	Raytheon (Hughes)
Country of manufacture:	USA
Diameter:	8in (203mm)
Span:	3ft 4in (1.02m)
Length:	12ft (3.66m)
Weight:	Up to 504lb (229kg)
Max Speed:	Mach 3.5
Range:	30 miles+ (48km+)

The original AIM-7A Sparrow I air-to-air missile began development by Sperry in the early mid 1940s and was a very different, primitive missile compared to the all-aspect, all-weather and all-altitude AIM-7 Sparrow currently in service.

The AIM-7A entered service in the mid 1950s and was guided using beam-riding technology. The Douglas AIM-7B Sparrow II with active radar was cancelled by the US Navy, continued by the Canadians who subsequently also

The AIM-9 Sidewinder (on the wing-tip) and AIM-7 Sparrow (under the wing) are common companions to provide short- and medium-range coverage. These missiles are on a Canadian Air Force CF-118A Hornet.

cancelled. The Raytheon AIM-7C Sparrow III commenced development in the mid 1950s, using semi-active radar homing guidance and was ordered for the US Navy. The AIM-7D replaced the solid motor with a liquid one. It was ordered for the US Navy and also the USAF as the AIM-101. The AIM-7E returned to solid fuel and became the basis for a number of variants. The AIM-7E2 was optimized for short-range with increased manoeuvrability, while in Italy the E was developed into the Aspide and in the UK the Sky Flash. It was also developed into the RIM-7H Sea Sparrow for use as a SAM on US Navy warships. The AIM-7F was fitted with solid-state electronics as well as a more powerful engine and larger continuous rod warhead; General Dynamics Pomona was contracted as a second source. The RIM-7F Sea Sparrow was also developed from this model.

Production continued with the AIM-7M inverse processed digital monopulse semi-active radar seeker which was similar to that fitted to the British Sky Flash. This greatly improved the capability of the Sparrow. It is also fitted with a blast/fragmentation warhead. The AIM-7P continued the improvements, especially at low level for use against missiles. It also saw the introduction of a command link. The AIM-7R combined the SARH head with multimode IR to reduce the effect of jamming targets. The RIM-7R Sea Sparrow was produced as a sub-variant. In addition, the Sparrow was also the basis for the AGM-45 Shrike anti-radar missile.

During the Gulf War, a total of twenty-five Iraqi aircraft were shot down using the AIM-7 Sparrow missile.

Having been in service for so long, the Sparrow has been built in large numbers, with over 34,000 built of just the AIM-7A, B, C, D and E models alone. The current models have been cleared for use on the F-4, F-14, F-15, F-16, F-104 and the F/A-18, and are used by US and a number of other air arms around the world including Canada, Italy, Portugal, Spain and Turkey.

TYPE:	AIM-9 SIDEWINDER

Manufacturer:	Raytheon/Loral
Country of manufacture:	USA
Diameter:	5in (120mm)
Span:	2ft 1in (630mm)
Length:	9ft 5in (2.8m)
Weight:	190lb (86kg)
Max speed:	Mach 2+
Range:	10 miles+ (16km+)

The design for the Sidewinder originated with the US Naval Weapons Center at China Lake in California during the late 1940s. The missile was first flown in 1953 and entered service in 1956. Its success was as a result of it being a simple missile, thus easy to build and inexpensive.

The AIM-9A was the prototype and did not enter production. The AIM-9B was only effective at very short ranges and only capable of detecting a target with an aspect ration of +/–30 degrees. It required the target to be immediately ahead and tail-on to give the IR seeker a usable reading. Considering the technology available, the Philco IR seeker, which included vacuum tubes and fitted in a 5in (120mm) diameter body, it was state of the art. Over 100,000 were built for US and European armed forces. The second generation AIM-9C was a semi-active radar seeker version for the US Navy built by Motorola, while the more successful AIM-9D was built by Ford. In 1982, a

An inert practice/drill AIM-9M Sidewinder with the double delta canard control fins fitted to a USAF A-10A Thunderbolt 2. On the next pylon is an AGM-65 Maverick which is also inert. Although they do not have warheads they are still used for operational training as the sensors are able to lock on to targets.

BELOW: The AIM-9D Sidewinder was initially used by the RAF on their Phantoms before the arrival of the -9L. Here, ground crew in NBC clothing prepare the live missiles during an exercise. The nose caps not only protect the lens but also contain a magnet to prevent damage to the gimbal. The unusual rollerons that spin in the slipstream provide a stabilizing a gyroscopic force.

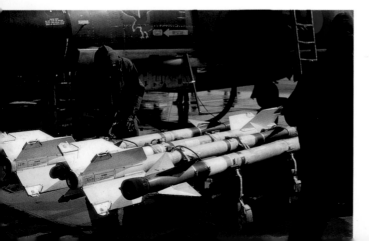

programme was initiated to produce a modification for existing surplus AIM-9C missiles for the anti-radiation role. These entered service in 1989 as the AGM-122A Sidearm. The AIM-9E was developed for the USAF with a wider angle and more effective seeker, and many earlier B models were upgraded. The US Navy AIM-9G incorporated an improved D model seeker and was soon eclipsed by the AIM-9H which featured an off-boresight lock-on capability and solid-state electronics. It also introduced the double delta forward control fins, which gave extra manoeuvrability. The AIM-9J was as the rebuilt B and E models with improved electronics and the double delta fins.

The next generation AIM-9L used a new seeker which now was capable of all-aspect targeting. The sensor is capable of detecting heat generated by air friction on the leading edge and fuselage of aircraft, but this technology came at a cost as it required a high degree of cooling. Nitrogen was used, but this meant that the missiles could not be left switched on for any length of time and required a warm-up period once switched on before they were effective. It also had the longer-span pointed fins and was armed with a blast/fragmentation warhead which was also surrounded by a layer of rods designed to shred the target. The 'Lima', as it was known, was also designed to have a substantial shelf life, as well as a substantial length life when fitted on to an aircraft. US production commenced in 1976 followed by European licence production in the early 1980s. In 1982 the RAF and Royal Navy were embroiled in conflict with the Argentinians over the Falkland Islands, but the European 'Lima' had yet to enter service. As a result, the US supplied 100 from its own stocks and some twenty-five Argentinian aircraft were brought down by these missiles.

The AIM-9M followed with the ability to ignore flares fired by the target to distract the missile. It was built in substantial numbers by various manufacturers for most NATO countries and is still in service in quantity on a wide variety of aircraft. The AIM-9N is the further improved J model, of which many were exported, and the AIM-9P was further improved B, E and J models plus new production. Work commenced on the AIM-9R, which was to feature further improvements of the M model, but work on this was stopped. The AIM-9S is similar to the AIM-9M, but fitted with a more powerful warhead.

The AIM-9X continues the development of the Sidewinder family when Raytheon was awarded the Naval Air Systems Command contract in a winner-take-all contract for the engineering, manufacture and development phase of the programme in December 1996. Although similar in appearance and using the same rocket motor which now incorporates thrust vectoring and warhead as the previous models to keep the costs down, the original -9X design commenced by Hughes Missile Systems (now part of Raytheon), incorporated a new advanced IR seeker developed for ASRAAM which 'sees' the whole target image

The AIM-9J, N and P models all featured the square-tipped canard control fins. The other items are used for producing smoke during aerobatic displays by an F-16 Fighting Falcon.

and can select the portion of the target to hit, as well as reducing its susceptibility to countermeasures.

The first guided launch of an AIM-9X was made by an F/A-18 Hornet on 1 June 1999. Once in service it will arm the USAF F-15C/E, F-16 and F-22 as well as the USN/USMC F/A-18 Hornet. USAF plans are for 5,080 missiles and the USN 5,000 over 17 years. The initial low-rate production contract was placed in November 2000.

BGT of Germany designed a modification kit for existing AIM-9J, N and P models to the 'Lima' standard and these are designated AIM-9JULI. Several versions of the AIM-9 have been built as a surface-to-air variant designated the MIM-72 Chaparral for the US Army.

The AIM-9 Sidewinder is used by over forty nations worldwide including all of the current NATO countries with the exception of the recently joined Eastern European countries. It has been or is still carried by a large range of aircraft including the A-4, A-6, A-7, A-10, F-4, F-5, F-14, F-15, F-16, F/A-18, F-20, F-104, F-111, Harrier, Hawk, JA 37 Viggen, Jaguar, Kfir, OV-10, MiG-21, Mirage 3, Mirage F1, Mitsubishi F-1, Nimrod MR.2, Sea Harrier, Tornado F.3, Tornado GR.1/4, as well as the AH-64A Apache and AH-1 Cobra helicopters.

BELOW: Fitted to the wing-tip of a US Navy F/A-18F Super Hornet is the AIM-9X which is the current production model of the Sidewinder and features thrust vectoring.

Manufacturer:	Raytheon (Hughes)
Country of manufacture:	USA
Diameter:	15in (380mm)
Span:	3ft (920mm)
Length:	13ft (3.96m)
Weight:	983lb (446kg)
Range:	83 miles (134km)

The AIM-54 Phoenix long-range air-to-air missile was developed in the the early 1960s by Hughes to arm the US Navy F-111B, which was subsequently cancelled in 1967. The development continued and Phoenix was transferred to the F-14 Tomcat project together with the AWG-9 radar. A Tomcat fired the first Phoenix in April 1972 and it entered service with the US Navy in 1974. The radar is capable of detecting targets at least 133 miles (213km) away and directing all six missiles at different targets simultaneously. The AIM-54 is guided to the target, which is illuminated by the AWG-9 radar in the F-14. When it is within 10 miles (16km) of the target, it switches on its own active radar guidance for the final phase of the attack. In addition to attacking enemy aircraft the AIM-54 can be used to destroy enemy cruise missiles.

Other variants of the Phoenix missile include the AIM-54B, which utilized a simpler construction technique in an attempt to reduce the cost of the $US 1 million missile. The AIM-54C entered service in 1985 and featured digital guidance and a solid-state radar. Besides these improvements, its range was increased to 92 miles (148km) and incorporated an improved proximity fuse.

A total of 2,566 AIM-54 Phoenix missiles were built and they are only carried by the F-14 Tomcat, which is currently in service with the US Navy.

A number of modified AIM-54s were sold to Iran to arm its F-14s, but it is thought that few, if any, remain in service. Six AIM-54 missiles can be carried by the F-14, but they are more likely to carry a mixture of long-, medium- and short-range missiles including AIM-7 Sparrow and AIM-9 Sidewinder missiles.

ABOVE: Armourers wheel an AIM-54 Phoenix across the carrier deck to a waiting F-14 Tomcat.

BELOW: An F-14A Tomcat of the PMTC launches an AIM-54 Phoenix missile. (Photo Raytheon via API)

AIM-120 AMRAAM Missile

Manufacturer:	Raytheon
Country of manufacture:	USA
Diameter:	7in (178mm)
Span:	17.6in (447mm)
Length:	12ft (3.65m)
Weight:	345lb (157kg)
Max speed:	Mach 4
Range:	31 miles (50km)

The Advanced Medium-Range Air-to-Air Missile (AMRAAM) was developed in the late 1970s under joint sponsorship with the USAF and US Navy by Hughes to replace the AIM-7 Sparrow. It is a medium-range, all-aspect, look-down, shoot-down, fire-and-forget air-to-air missile with a multiple launch capability. It is an all-weather missile and can be launched day or night at targets Beyond Visual Range (BVR). It has a fast launch, is resistant to countermeasures and has a good low-level attack capability.

Powered by an Alliant 45 low smoke motor, the AIM-120 uses an active radar guidance and incorporates the latest digital technology and micro-miniaturized solid-state electronics, resulting in a missile which is significantly more reliable and maintainable. On launching, the missile is guided by its inertial navigation and then receives updated co-ordinates from the launch aircraft mid-course and then uses its own active radar seeker during the final stage of the intercept. Once the missile has been launched the aircraft is able to turn from the engaged target to attack another. The first AIM-120 was launched in December 1984 and deliveries commenced in 1988.

The AIM-120B represents an upgrade model for export with improved seeker and warhead capabilities. The AIM-120C is powered by an Alliant enhanced rocket motor which gives an extra 13 per cent increase in performance. It also features clipped wing to enable it to be carried by the F-22.

USAF ground crew check an AIM-120 AMRAAM and an AIM-9M Sidewinder on an F-16 Fighting Falcon of the 31st FW at Aviano AFB in Italy prior to a CAP mission over the former Yugoslavia.

The AIM-120 was used operationally during missions over Iraq, when two aircraft were shot down out of three missiles fired. In Kosovo three Serbian MiG-29 were also shot down with AIM-120 missiles.

The AIM-120 AMRAAM is being used to replace the Sky Flash missile on the RAF Tornado F.3 and will be carried by the Eurofighter. It is fitted to the Royal Navy Sea Harrier FA.2 as well as the USAF F-15 and F-16 and the German Air Force F-4F Phantom. It will be carried by the F-22, while the US Navy currently uses them on the F-14 and F/A-18. The AMRAAM is used by twenty air forces throughout the world including those of a number of NATO members. AMRAAM has also been developed into several SAM programmes.

AIM-132 ASRAAM Missile

Manufacturer:	MBDA (Matra BAe Dynamics)
Country of manufacture:	UK
Diameter:	6.5in (166mm)
Length:	9ft 6in (2.9m)
Weight:	192lb (87kg)
Range:	6.2 miles (10km)

The Advanced Short-Range Air-to-Air Missile (ASRAAM) was originally conceived as a joint France/Germany/UK/USA missile project back in the early 1980s. A Memorandum of

Understanding (MoU) was signed in 1982 which agreed that Europe would design the ASRAAM with co-production in the USA as the AIM-132, while the AMRAAM would be vice versa. As various hurdles were encountered the consortium gradually lost its members. France went on to build the MICA, Germany is developing the IRIS-T and the USA the AIM-9X, leaving the UK to carry on with the project alone.

In 1992 a contract was given to British Aerospace to develop and produce the first 1,000

AIR-TO-AIR WEAPONS

11

A mock-up of the ASRAAM on a mock-up of the SAAB Gripen.

missiles. The first guided firing was made from an F-16 in 1996, with the contract specifying a total of fourteen required to demonstrate the capabilities of the ASRAAM. In 1998 the RAAF selected ASRAAM to be fitted to its Hornets during their upgrade. The USAF evaluated the ASRAAM to compete with the AIM-9X but it was not selected.

ASRAAM is powered by a solid rocket motor and features a fast launch and high agility for use in a close combat scenario. It is capable of attacking any aircraft within the pilot's visual range using co-ordinates from the pilot's helmet-mounted sight or the aircraft's systems. It is also capable of operating as a stand-alone missile using its own IR seeker.

A variant of the ASRAAM has been proposed. Named the Typhoon, this model of the air-to-air missile may be developed for the anti-armour role.

The ASRAAM will be fitted to the Harrier GR.7, Tornado F.3 and Typhoon of the RAF and the Sea Harrier FA.2 of the Royal Navy. Deliveries of pre-production missiles were made in 1998 for training purposes. A total of four variants will be delivered to the RAF. The operational round is delivered in a sealed container until required for use. There is a live training missile that has telemetry installed instead of a warhead, enabling a full evaluation of the flight to be conducted after firing. There is also an acquisition round that has the seeker and can carry out the whole launch sequence up to the actual firing. The final variant is an inert training round that is used for training ground crew in the correct ground handling and loading procedures.

TYPE: ASPIDE 1, 2000 (MK.30) MISSILE

Manufacturer:	MBDA (Alenia Marconi)
Country of manufacture:	Italy
Diameter:	8in (203mm)
Span:	26.77in (680mm)
Length:	12.14ft (3.7m)
Weight:	531lb (241kg)
Max speed:	High supersonic
Range:	12.4 miles+ (20km+)

Development of the Aspide was begun in the early 1970s by Selenia, initially as a private venture to replace the Sparrow missiles in service with the Italian Air Force F-104 Starfighters. It was also designed with a multirole capability. As a naval SAM it was part of the Albatross system, while a ground-launched SAM model was incorporated in the Spada and the Skyguard-Aspide air defence systems.

While the SAM variants entered service in the late 1970s, difficulties led to delays so that the Aspide 1 only entered service with the Italian Air Force in 1988. Work commenced on an Aspide 2, but this halted when the Italian Air Force joined the European Meteor programme. In the early 1990s a new model referred to as the Aspide 2000 or Mk.30 emerged with a revised design. Externally, the body diameter was increased from the original 203mm to accommodate a more powerful motor and the wing and tail surface shape was also revised. Various other internal improvements have also been made including an improved seeker.

A production Aspide Mk.30 in test.
(Photo Alenia Marconi via API)

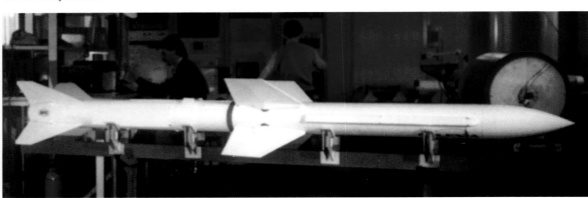

Manufacturer:	Raytheon (General Dynamics)
Country of manufacture:	USA
Diameter:	2.75in (70mm)
Span:	3.55in (90mm)
Length:	5ft (1.52m)
Weight:	34.5lb (15.7kg)
Max speed:	Supersonic
Range:	4.5 miles (7.2km)

General Dynamics began development on the Stinger in the early 1970s as a surface-to-air missile, initially as the FIM-92 Man-Portable Air Defence System (MANPADS) to replace the Redeye missile. The development of the air-to-air variant began in the mid 1980s and entered service in 1988.

Stinger is a short-range air defence missile which uses a two-colour – infrared/ultra-violet – detector together with advanced algorithms, enabling it to disregard countermeasures by the target. Stinger is capable of being fired by a soldier from a shoulder launcher, a vehicle or a helicopter. It has a fire-and-forget capability for use against helicopters, fixed-wing aircraft, UAV and cruise missiles.

A number of models of the Stinger missile have been built over the years. The FIM-92A was purely a ground-launched missile. The FIM-92B POST

The Stinger will also arm the RAH-66 Comanche and a pair can be seen located in the weapons bay between a pair of Hellfire missiles.

featured improved sensor and counter-countermeasure capabilities. The FIM-92C Stinger RMP (Reprogrammable Micro-Processor) incorporates advanced technology to enable it to continue its high hit success rate of over 90 per cent. In development is the 3PI programme (Pre-Planned Product Improvement), which will include hardware and software changes. This enables the missile software to be easily updated as new threats are encountered, and they can be used in the SAM or air-to-air role. The FIM-92D

During the Gulf War, Stinger missiles were used by all four US forces to provide area protection for a wide range of sites, ranging from troop manoeuvres to Patriot missile launchers.

The FIM-92 was proposed for use on fixed aircraft such as the B-52, but has only been cleared for use on helicopters such as the AH-1, AH-64, OH-58, Tiger, UH-60. They will be fitted to the RAH-66. The Stinger missile has seen widespread use, with over 60,000 having been ordered. Besides the US armed forces, customers include Denmark, France, Italy, Germany, Greece, the Netherlands and Turkey, although only some may be in use in the air-to-air role.

An FIM-92 Stinger fitted to a US Army OH-58D Kiowa Warrior.

Manufacturer:	MBDA (Matra BAe Dynamics)
Country of manufacture:	France
Diameter:	6.3in (160mm)
Length:	10.17ft (3.10m)
Weight:	247lb (112kg)
Range:	37 miles (60km)

The development of the MICA (*Missile d'Interception et de Combat et d'Autodéfence* – dogfight/self-defence/interception missile) by Matra began in 1982 with the intention of being able to replace the short-range Magic and medium-range Super 530D with a single high capability missile.

AIR-TO-AIR WEAPONS

13

ABOVE: A display showing the MICA EM (top) and the MICA IR (bottom).

RIGHT: An inert variant variant of MICA which is cleared for flight by the French Air Force and designated MICA EMP.

The MICA has the option of an active radar guidance (MICA ER) or infrared sensor (MICA IR) capability through interchangeable heads. The IR sensor can remain active for the whole flight, providing the pilot with additional discrete monitoring capability. Once launched, the missile is autonomous, allowing the pilot to launch further missiles at other targets. The MICA ER was the first to be developed, and the first flight using its guidance control was made in 1991.

While the MICA has a good all-round capability, its weight is on the heavy side for close-up high manoeuvring compared to some short-range missiles. A reduced size variant was offered to meet UK and German short-range missile requirements, but these countries rejected it in favour of their own ASRAAM and IRIS-T systems. A vertical-launched Mica had also been proposed for SHOrt RAnge Air Defence (SHORAD).

MICA ER has already been exported to Taiwan and Qatar and both the ER and IR variants are about to enter service with the French Air Force on their Mirage 2000-5, and will also be used by UAE and Greek Air Force on delivery of their Mirages. The MICA will also be used to arm the Rafale of the French Air Force and Navy.

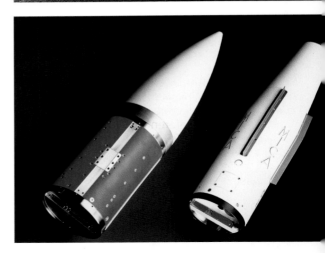

Close-up of the interchangeable homing heads for the MICA missiles. (Photo Matra Défense via API)

TYPE: MISTRAL **ATAM** MISSILE

Manufacturer:	MBDA (Matra BAe Dynamics)
Country of manufacture:	France
Diameter:	3.54in (90mm)
Length:	6.1ft (1.86m)
Weight:	43lb (19.5kg)
Max speed:	Mach 2.5

The ATAM (Air-to-Air Mistral) was developed from the Mistral. This short-range IR missile system was designed as a SAM for use as a shoulder-launched, vehicle- or ship-mounted missile by Matra in the 1970s. It was part of the specifica-

tion that the missile should be common to each of the systems and the French Army was the first recipient in 1988.

Initially referred to as the *Helicoptère Air Trés Courtre Portée* (HATCP) missile, development of the air-to-air variant commenced in 1986. Although a quantity of ATAMs were made available for French Army Gazelles to use during the Gulf War in 1991, the missile did not become fully operational until 1994. The ATAM system comprises a pair of launchers either side of the helicopter, enabling four missiles to be carried. The seeker is able to detect and enable the missile to intercept aircraft and helicopters flying close to the ground at ranges up to 6,000m (6,562yd).

The ATAM system is designed so that it can be easily integrated with most types of helicopters to provide a self-defence capability. These helicopters can then be operated to provide escort for other helicopters or land forces. A variant known as Mistral 2 has been developed for use as a SAM.

Over 16,000 Mistral missiles have been sold to twenty-five countries and used by thirty-six air forces, armies and navies including Belgium, Norway and Spain. The ATAM is used by the French Army to arm its Gazelles, and clearance was given in July 1999 for the Tiger gunship which is on order for a number of NATO countries.

An ATAM mounted on a French Army Gazelle

Type:	R-3, R-13, R-131 (AA-2 'Atoll') Missile

Manufacturer:	Vympel (Turopov)
Country of manufacture:	Russia
Diameter:	5in (127mm)
Span:	1.74ft (530mm)
Length:	9.28ft (2.83m)
Weight:	198lb (90kg)

The AA-2 'Atoll' missile was first revealed in 1961 when it was seen fitted to Russian aircraft at an airshow. It had been in development for a couple of years and appears to use the American AIM-9B Sidewinder as the reference.

As with the AIM-9B, the AA-2 had a IR heat-seeking head, but towards the end of the decade a longer (3.5m) variant with a SARH head was described as an 'Advanced Atoll' and

given the NATO designation AA-2C. Further improvements to the IR head continued, with production in large numbers continuing to around the mid 1980s.

The AA-2 has been fitted to the majority of Russian combat aircraft of the 1980s and 1990s including the MiG-19, MiG-21, MiG-23, MiG-27, Su-17/20 and Su-21 aircraft, in virtually all of the former Warsaw Pact and Russian-supported countries including the Czech Republic, Hungary and Poland.

BELOW: An AA-2A/R-3 fitted on a MiG-21 'Fishbed'. (Photo Ryszard Malachowski)

BOTTOM: An AA-2C/R13 (left) plus a part of R60/AA-8 on a MiG-21 'Fishbed'. (Photo Ryszard Malachowski)

R-23 (AA-7 'APEX') MISSILE

Manufacturer:	Vympel
Country of manufacture:	Russia
Diameter:	7.87in (200mm)
Span:	3.41ft (1.04m)
Length:	13.65ft (4.16m)
Weight:	518lb (235kg)
Range:	31 miles (50km)

The Russian R-23 missile was developed in the late 1960s as a medium-range air-to-air missile which was given the NATO codename AA-7 'Apex'. This missile was built with either infrared or semi-active radar seekers; later improved variants were designated R-24.

The R-23 is carried by MiG-23, MiG-25 and MiG-29 and was reported as having been used by Iraq during its war with neighbouring Iran. Most operators of these aircraft have the R-23 in their inventory including the Polish and Czech Air Forces.

An R-23 with a semi-active radar guidance head fitted to a MiG-23. (Photo Stephen Wolf/API)

R-27 (AA-10 'ALAMO') MISSILE

Manufacturer:	Vympel
Country of manufacture:	Russia
Diameter:	9.06in (230mm)
Span:	2.62ft (800mm)
Length:	14.76 (4.50m)
Weight:	756lb (343kg)
Range:	74.5 miles (120km)

The Russian R-27 was given the NATO code and reporting name AA-10 'Alamo'. The development stems from the mid 1970s and resulted in a family of missiles, the earlier of which probably entered service in the mid 1980s. The R-27 variants basically fall into two categories – IR or radar guidance. The IR guidance is identified by a lens on the blunt nose, while the radar-guided variant

An R-27T missile with the IR seeker on a Su-35.

The R-27ER with a semi-active radar seeker on a MiG-21.

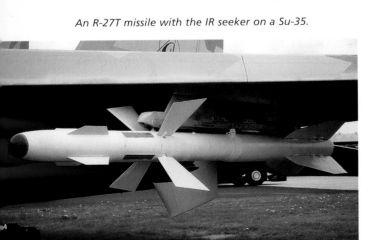

has a solid pointed nose. Within each of these categories are medium-, long- and extended-range missiles, and the radar-guided model comes with active or semi-active radar, although the noses look similar. The range of the missiles is reflected in their length.

The R-27 is a modular missile comprising three section – nose, tail and centre fuselage. The basic type is readily identifiable by its unique butterfly-like canard control surfaces on the centre section which also includes the autopilot and battery. The nose section is easily identified by the two types

The improved R-27R1.

The R-73 was first seen on the MiG-29 and Su-27, but it can probably be fitted to the MiG-21, MiG-23, MiG-25, Su-30MK and Su-35. It is probable that many operators of these aircraft have included variants of the R-27 in their inventories including the Czech, Hungarian and Polish Air Forces.

of seeker nose, while the tail section which contains the motor has a long or short section of fuselage reflecting the amount of fuel carried.

The following models are believed to have been developed: R-27T medium-range IR; R-27ET extended-range IR; R-27ET1 improved medium-range all-aspect IR; R-27R medium-range semi-active radar; R-27ER extended-range semi-active radar; R-27ER1 improved extended-range semi-active radar; R-27EM long-range semi-active radar modified for low-level interception; R-27AE extended-range active radar; R-27P passive radar seeker; and R-23EP extended-range passive radar seeker

The improved R-27ET1.

TYPE: R-40, R-46RD (AA-6 'ACRID') MISSILE

Manufacturer:	Spetztechnika
Country of manufacture:	Russia
Diameter:	13.98in (355mm)
Span:	5.91ft (1.8m)
Length:	20.34ft (6.2m)
Weight:	1,041lb (472kg)
Range:	31 miles (50km)

The development of the R-40 air-to-air missile commenced in the late 1960s and was allocated the NATO reporting designation of AA-6 'Acrid'. The R-40 has been built in two forms – the R-40T with an IR seeker and the R-40R which has a semi-active radar guidance. It would appear that the R-40R was unsatisfactory as it has only

been seen on rare occasions, while the R-40T has been displayed and seen fitted to a number of aircraft. The R-40T has also been the subject of a number of improvement programmes with subsequent models being designated R-40D and R-40D1. The latest improvement resulted in the R-46, which entered service in the early 1980s for the MiG-31.

The R-40 has been seen fitted to a number of aircraft including the Su-22m, MiG-25 and MiG-31, and continues to be in service with operators of these aircraft including the Hungarian and Polish Air Forces.

The IR variant of the R-40/R-46.

R-60 (AA-8 'APHID') MISSILE

Manufacturer:	Spetztekhnika
Country of manufacture:	Russia
Diameter:	5.12in (130mm)
Span:	17in (430mm)
Length:	6.82ft (2.08m)
Weight:	139lb (63kg)
Range:	1.8 miles (3km)

Development of the R-60 short-range air-to-air missile began at the end of the 1960s; it was allocated the NATO reporting designation of AA-8 'Aphid'. It was first seen in the West in 1976 and is believed to exist only with an IR seeker. It has since been seen on a wide number of aircraft such as the MiG-21, MiG-23, MiG-25, MiG-29 and MiG-31, as well as the Su-22, Su-24, Su-27. Reports also include the Mi-24 and the Romanian Air Force Puma.

During the early 1980s the continued development resulted in an improved model designated R-60M followed by the R-60MK.

The R-60 continues to be operated by the

A mock-up of the R-60 on a Georgian Air Force Su-25.

various operators of Russian-built aircraft including the Czech, Hungarian and Polish Air Forces.

R-73 (AA-11 'ARCHER') MISSILE

Manufacturer:	Vympel
Country of manufacture:	Russia
Diameter:	6.69in (170mm)
Span:	1.67ft (510mm)
Length:	9.51ft (2.9m)
Weight:	231lb (105kg)
Range:	18.6 miles (30km)

An R-73.

The Vympel R-73 air-to-air missile was developed during the 1970s/1980s and entered service towards the end of the 1980s and was allocated the NATO designation AA-11 'Archer'. It utilizes an all-aspect IR seeker and can accept target designation from any aircraft systems including the IRST and helmet-mounted sights. It features vanes in the exhaust to provide thrust vectoring together with conven-

tional control surfaces on the wings. This enables a high off-boresight of 45 degrees; however, an improved variant has increased this to 60 degrees. The R-73 can be fitted with an active radar fuse or active laser to enable detonation in proximity of the target in addition to a contact fuse.

A pair of R-73s on a Su-35.

The R-73 has been cleared to operate from most Russian combat aircraft and serves with most of the former Warsaw Pact air forces including Czech, Germany, Hungary and Poland.

TYPE:	R.530 MISSILE

Manufacturer:	Aerospatiale Matra
Country of manufacture:	France
Diameter:	10.35in (263mm)
Span:	3.61ft (1.1m)
Length:	10.5ft (3.2m)
Weight:	427lb (193.5kg)
Max speed:	Mach 2.7
Range:	11 miles (18km)

The R.530 air-to-air missile development was begun in the mid 1950s by Matra.

The R.530 was produced with two interchangeable seeker heads. The IR model is recognized by the nose-mounted lens. The other is

The R.530 with an IR seeker on a French Air Force Mirage F.1.

The Semi-Active Radar version of the R.530.

the Semi-Active Radar (SAR), which was slightly longer – 3.28m (10.8ft) – and had an opaque nose.

Over 4,000 R.530 missiles for fourteen nations were built, but were subsequently replaced by the Super 530 and may only remain in limited service. The R.530 was cleared for use on the Mirage III, F.1 and F-8E (FN).

Manufacturer:	MBDA (Matra)
Country of manufacture:	France
Diameter:	6.18in (157mm)
Span:	2.17ft (660mm)
Length:	9.02ft (2.75m)
Weight:	196lb (89kg)
Max speed:	Mach 2.0+
Range:	12.4 miles (20km)

An R.550 Magic 2 missile on a French Air Force Mirage 2000N.

The Magic air-to-air missile commenced as a private venture by Matra to compete with the AIM-9 Sidewinder during the mid 1960s. The first guided launch was made in 1972 and initial deliveries to the French Air Force began two years later.

As with the early Sidewinder missiles, the R.550 Magic 1 was limited by the sensitivity of the IR seeker to tail-aspect attacks. Powered by a solid motor rocket, it was designed to be interchangeable with the Sidewinder.

The Magic saw considerable success with orders exceeding 6,000 missiles and deliveries to some twenty-seven countries including France, Greece, Portugal and Spain.

Further development of the Magic 1 in the late 1970s led to a far more superior seeker, and as such the Magic 2 entered service with the French Air Force in 1985. This was an all-aspect missile similar in size to the earlier Magic 1, but with increased speed and range as well as the guid-ance which is also resistant to countermeasures. An active Doppler radar fuze has replaced the proximity activated one.

In 1995 the Magic 2 Mk.2 entered service with further improvements to the IF homing head technology and manoeuvrability. The maximum range was increased from 15km (9.3 miles) to over 20km (12.4 miles).

The Magic 2 is used by the French Air Force and Navy on their Mirage 2000, and F.1 as well as the Jaguar and Super Etendard, and exports have been made to a number of countries including the Belgian Air Force. Production for Magic 1 and 2 totals over 11,000 missiles in use or on order with nineteen countries throughout the world.

TYPE: **SKY FLASH MISSILE**

Manufacturer:	**MBDA (BAe)**
Country of manufacture:	UK
Diameter:	8in (203mm)
Span:	3.35ft (1.02m)
Length:	12ft (3.66m)
Weight:	430lb (195kg)
Max speed:	Mach 2+
Range:	25 miles+ (40km+)

The Sky Flash medium-range air-to-air missile was developed in the UK from the AIM-7E Sparrow to ensure full compatibility with the RAF Phantoms, on which four were normally fitted.

The Sky Flash featured a semi-active guidance seeker that would detect reflected radiation from the aircraft radar system. Following the introduction of the Tornado F.3 into RAF service and the withdrawal of the Phantom, the Sky Flash underwent a modification programme to improve it and to make it compatible with Tornado F.3. This was referred to as the Tornado Essential Modification Programme (TEMP). Subsequent further improvements have resulted in the Super-TEMP Sky Flash.

On the Tornado F.3 the Sky Flash missiles are carried on Frazer-Nash Launchers, which are recessed into the underside of the fuselage. This launcher ejects the missile away from the aircraft when fired. A total of four Sky Flash missiles can be carried on the Tornado F.3.

The Sky Flash has been cleared to use with the Phantom, Tornado, F-16 and Viggen. It is used by the RAF and exports have been made to Sweden and some Middle East countries.

An RAF Sky Flash, with the blue circles indicating that it is an inert training model.

Manufacturer:	Lockheed Martin/Short
Country of manufacture:	UK/USA
Diameter:	5.12in (130mm)
Span:	9.75in (250mm)
Length:	4ft 7in (1.40m)
Weight:	35lb (16kg)
Range:	3 miles+ (5km+)

Feasibility studies for the Shorts Starstreak missile commenced in 1980, eventually leading to a development contract and initial production from the Ministry of Defence in 1986.

Starstreak is a Hyper Velocity Missile (HVM) which was designed as a surface-to-air missile. The body of the missile contains a two-stage motor together with a guidance control data-linked to the launcher. Starstreak does not require seeker cooling and so can be launched immediately a target is acquired. The first motor boosts the missile to Mach 3 in 0.9 seconds and is then ejected after some 400m (1,300ft) when the second stage takes over. Mounted at the front inside the structure of the missile are three darts that are ejected when the motor burns out. These beamride to the target and contain a small HE charge to enhance the damage when they hit the target.

In 1988 a teaming agreement was made with McDonnell Douglas to develop an air-to-air missile variant – Helstreak – for use on US Army AH-64 Apache and later referred to as the Air-To-Air Starstreak (ATASK). Lockheed Martin joined the team in 1989 and it is currently in competition with the FIM-92 Stinger for the US Army contract.

In the meantime, Starstreak is in service with the British Army as a surface-to-air missile fitted to the Alvis Stormer and as a shoulder-launched missile. The US Army commenced trials fitting Starstreak to an Avenger vehicle, but these were abandoned in 1994. A further application to fit the missile to ships has resulted in the development of the Seastreak variant.

Starstreak is in production and is to be fitted to the British Army AH-64 Longbow Apaches.

The Starstreak, showing the three darts.
(Photo Shorts via API)

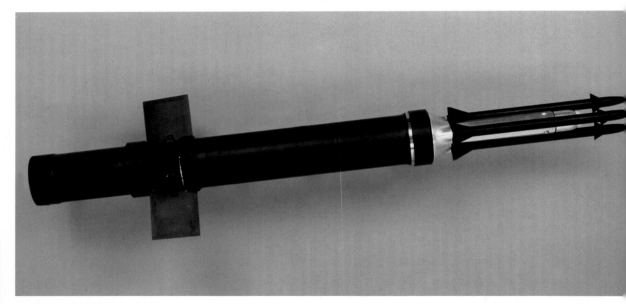

Manufacturer:	MBDA (Aerospatiale Matra)
Country of manufacture:	France
Diameter:	10.35in (263mm)
Span:	2.1ft (640mm)
Length:	11.6ft (3.54m)
Weight:	551lb (250kg)
Max speed:	Mach 4.6
Range:	22 miles (35km)

The ancestry of the Super 530 medium-range air-to-air missile can be traced back to the Matra R.530 which entered service in the early 1960s, but it is actually of a vastly superior design and performance.

The Super 530F uses a SARH seeker (no IR variant was built) which relies on the Cyrano IV radar fitted to the Mirage F1 to provide the tar-

get illumination. The first fully functioning Super 530F flight took place in 1974 and they entered service in 1979 with the French Air Force and became the standard weapon for the Mirage F1C. The Super 530F proved to be a powerful missile capable of snap-up climb of 9,000m (29,500ft) and acceleration to Mach 4.6. In 1984 production commenced of the

A Super 530 on a French Air Force Mirage 2000.

Super 530D. This featured a monopulse continuous wave doppler semi-active radar which used the RDI radar fitted to the Mirage 2000 to be able to track and attack low-flying targets.

The Super 530 missiles have been cleared on the Mirage F.1 2000 and Rafale.

57MM S-5 ROCKET

Manufacturer:	Vympel/Kokintex
Country of manufacture:	Russia/Poland/Romania
Diameter:	2.2in (55mm)
Length:	3.28ft (1m)
Weight:	8.8lb (4kg)

The 57mm S-5 rocket is thought to have developed roughly in parallel with the US 2.75in (70mm) rocket, with origins around the late 1940s. Over the years a number of purpose-designed warheads have evolved to enable their use against various targets together with improvements in motor performance. It is thought that the S-5 has been built in greater numbers than any other rocket. In addition, a variant of the Russian 57mm S-5 rocket was also

The 16 57mm S-5 rockets with a UB-16-57 rocket launcher pod.

The 32 rocket UB-32-57 rocket launcher pod.

developed and built locally for use by the Bulgarian and Romanian armed forces.

The S-5 rockets are normally carried in UB-8-57, UB-16-57, UB-19-57 and UB-32-57 rocket launcher pods with the middle number indicating the rocket capacity. They can be carried by a range of Russian and Eastern European operated aircraft and helicopters including the IAR-93 Orao, IAR-99 Soim, IAR-330L Puma, L-39ZA Albatros, Mi-2, Ka-50, Ka-52, Mi-8 /17, Mi-24/35, MiG-AT, MiG-21, MiG-23, Su-22 and Su-25.

The S-5 remains widely used by the former Warsaw Pact armed forces and is operational within NATO carried by a number of the aircraft of the Czech, Hungarian and Polish armed forces.

68MM MULTI-DART ROCKETS

Manufacturer:	TDA/FZ
Country of manufacture:	France
Diameter:	2.68in (68mm)
Span:	9.45in (240mm)

The 68mm Multi-Dart rocket system was developed during the late 1970s by Thomson Brandt as an extension to their range of earlier and successful 68mm rockets. At the same time, work was also being carried out on a similar range of the heavier 100mm (4in) rockets.

The Multi-Dart system comprises a rocket of similar dimension to the standard 68mm rocket but is fitted with a more powerful rocket motor to increase the range and impact velocity. Two variants are produced – the AMV and the ABL. The AMV contains thirty-six kinetic energy darts which separate from the rocket as a pre-set time giving them time to spread and saturate the target area. The AMV is effective against equipment and vehicles.

The ABL comprises eight kinetic energy darts which are effective against light armoured vehicles.

Three 68mm Multi-Dart launcher pods are available – the LR-68-8, LR-68-12 and the LR-68-22 with the last number indicating the number of rockets that can be accommodated.

68mm Multi-Dart rockets with an LR-68-12 launcher pod.

Manufacturer:	TDA (Thomson Brandt)
Country of manufacture:	France
Diameter:	2.68in (68mm)
Length:	2.03ft (620mm)
Weight (empty):	Up to 13.67lb (6.2kg)

The 68mm rocket was originally developed by Thomson Brandt in the early 1950s to provide the French armed forces with their own rocket that was similar to the US 2.75in system. Production commenced in the mid 1950s for the French Army and Air Force helicopters and strike aircraft. A number of warheads were developed to provide a range of capabilities and a number of launchers designed to enable a comprehensive capability for most requirements although a heavier 100mm (4in) rocket was developed in the mid 1960s.

These 68mm rockets were also known as SNEB and were widely used, with production running into millions. They are normally fired in ripples from the F-1 pod with thirty-six rounds or the F-2 with six rounds for fixed-wing aircraft or the F-4 with eighteen rounds for helicopters. These pods were all built by Matra. Thomson Brandt also built the 68-12 and 68-22 pods for helicopters with twelve and twenty-two rounds respectively.

ABOVE: The Type 155 pod is similar to the F4 but stressed for supersonic flight.

BELOW: An RAF Armourer loading 68mm SNEB rockets into a Type 155 launcher pod.

BELOW: These 68mm SNEB rockets are the contents of the two F4 launcher pods mounted on the helicopter stub wing.

The frangible cover enables the rockets to blast their way through.

In the latter 1970s, Thomson Brandt began development of a new 68mm rocket referred to as the Multi-Dart. This new rocket was designed specifically for use against armour and was basically the carrier of a number of small submunitions which spread out to form a rain of deadly projectiles each using kinetic energy to pierce 10mm of armour plate. Depending on the rocket model, there can be either eight or thirty-six of these projectiles. As the multi-dart rockets were longer than the original SNEBs additional launcher pods were designed by TDA, as the company was now known. Designated LR 68-8, LR 68-12, LR 68-22, the second number indicated the number of rounds carried. Matra produced a single new launcher with a capacity for eighteen rockets designated Type 155 and was stressed to be able to withstand supersonic flight.

The pods for the SNEB and Multi-Dart rockets have standard NATO lugs and can therefore be carried by a large number of aircraft and helicopters, and continue to serve with many NATO countries as well as armed forces throughout the world.

TYPE: 2.75IN (70MM) CRV7 ROCKET WEAPON SYSTEM

Manufacturer:	Magellan/Bristol
Country of manufacture:	Canada
Diameter:	9.84in (250mm)
Length:	5.31ft (1.62m)
Weight:	216lb (98kg)

Development of this Canadian rocket motor began in 1970 with the intention of producing a motor with improved performance and reliability over existing examples. The resulting CRV7 (Canadian Rocket Vehicle) is now produced with a permutation of motors and warheads that can be combined for specific roles. Compared to most other systems the rockets have a higher kinetic energy which enables them to fly a flatter trajectory, resulting in them flying further and with greater accuracy.

The CRV7 can be fitted into a number of launcher pods including the M260, M261, six-tube LAU-5002 and LAU-5005 and the nineteen-tube LAU-5003 (399mm diameter by 1.49m). The usual configuration is for nineteen of the multi-purpose 70mm (2.75in) rockets to be loaded in a

CRV7 rockets visible protruding out the front of an LAU 5002 launcher pod.

The RAF have taken delivery of a quantity of the six-round LAU 5002 launcher pods for training.

pod for use against area targets comprising of light armour and soft-skinned vehicles as well as personnel. These can be carried by a wide range of aircraft and helicopters. The data given is for the LAU-5002 displayed and the weight is approximate depending on the actual warheads fitted.

The CRV7 is one of the leading 2.75in unguided rocket weapon systems available today due to the greater stand-off distances, higher kinetic energy and superior accuracy to both fixed-wing and helicopter users. Almost 700,000 of these rockets have been produced. The CRV7 is in service in Canada and with various forces of NATO, ASEAN and Australasia. A number were fired from RAF Jaguars during the Gulf War and can be carried by the Harrier GR.7. They will also be one of the armaments of the RAF Typhoon when it enters service. Optimized for use on helicopters, the latest development of the CRV7, the C17 variant, has been chosen for the UK Apache Attack Helicopter program.

Manufacturer:	TDA (FZ)
Country of manufacture:	Belgium
Diameter:	2.75in (70mm)
Length:	various
Weight:	various

Forges of Zeebrugge (now TDA) build the US 2.75in (70mm) FFAR (Fin Folding Aircraft Rocket) under licence and have designed their own range of launch pods to be used with their improved rocket variants. The M157/A is a seven-tube launcher for helicopters and has three variants depending on the trigger fitted. The M159/A is a nineteen-tube launcher, again with three trigger-dependent variants for helicopters but has an optional rear removable fairing. The LAU 183 is another launcher designed for use by helicopters and houses twelve rockets. The LAU 32 has been designed for use by attack aircraft and has a fixed-shaped nose plus a removable rear fairing. Seven rockets can be fitted and there are three variants depending on the trigger mechanism. The LAU 51 launcher is also for aircraft use and accommodates nineteen rockets again in three variants.

A seven-round LAU 32.

Nineteen 70mm FZ rockets with the LAU 51 launcher pod.

A pair of the nineteen-round M159 launcher pods designed for helicopters.

Manufacturer:	BEI Defence/Alliant/General Dynamics
Country of manufacture:	USA
Diameter:	2.75in (70mm)
Span:	7.32in (186mm)
Length:	various
Weight:	various

The Hydra 70 rocket is the development of the 2.75in (70mm) rocket that has been in service with the US armed forces as well as numerous others around the world. These rockets have evolved from the original Mickey Mouse air-to-air rockets of the late 1940s. Development included the Mk 4 and Mk 40 rockets for fixed-wing aircraft and helicopters respectively. They were widely used during the Vietnam period and were often referred to as the Folding Fin Aircraft Rocket. Many are still in current service.

The US Navy instigated development of a further improvement which was designated the Mk.66 rocket which was to have improved range

and accuracy and incorporated a Wrap Around Fin Air Rocket (WAFAR). A range of components was developed to enable the rocket to be used for a variety of roles. These include various motors, warheads and fuzes enabling the rocket to be profiled for an individual mission. Four rocket launchers were developed for the Hydra 70 system. These are the seven-tube reusable LAU-68 D/A and the nineteen-tube reusable LAU-61 C/A.

In 1987, the Canadian Bristol Aerospace began development of two new motors for its existing CRV7 rocket system. As these were also 2.75in it was decided to make them fully compatible with the Hydra 70 System. In the late 1970s the US Army requested a new rocket launcher to house the Hydra rockets and these led to the M260 and M261 rocket launcher pods. Details of both of these systems are listed in their own right.

Over the years the Hydra 70 rocket system has been cleared for use on a large number of aircraft and helicopters including the A-4, A-6, A-7, AV-

2.75in Hydra 70 rockets protrude from an M260 launcher pod mounted on the stub wing of a USMC AH-1W SuperCobra. In front is a quadruple TOW launcher.

8B, A-10, AH-1F, AH-1T AH-1W, AH-64A, F-4, F-5 F-16, F/A-18 Hornet, F-104, Jaguar, OH-58/Scout, OV-10 Bronco, P-3 Orion and UH-1H Iroquois.

TYPE:	M260 ROCKET LAUNCHER POD

Manufacturer:	Harvard Interiors
Country of manufacture:	USA
Diameter:	10in (254mm)
Length:	5ft 6in (1.68m)
Weight (empty):	34lb (15.5kg)

The M260 is a lightweight rocket launcher pod designed for use with the 2.75in (70mm) Hydra 70 unguided rockets. They were initially designed by Hughes Aircraft to meet a US Army requirement for use on their AH-1 and AH-64 Apache attack helicopters. It features a system that enables the aircrew to adjust remotely the rocket fuze. The M260 houses a total of seven rockets, while the M261 pod that was developed at the same time carries nineteen rockets. Both pods were designed to be lighter than their predecessors and are simple in construction. They have a limited life of sixteen firings; apart from the rockets, they have no replaceable parts should they be damaged.

The seven-round M260 launcher pod.

Production commenced in 1979 and a total over 7,000 of the M260 and M261 pods were built for the US Army.

TYPE:	M261 ROCKET LAUNCHER POD

Manufacturer:	Harvard Interiors
Country of manufacture:	USA
Diameter:	16in (406mm)
Length:	5ft 6in (1.68m)
Weight (empty):	87.5lb (39.7kg)

The nineteen-round M261 rocket launcher pod mounted on a British Army WAH-64D Longbow Apache. Inboard is a quad Hellfire launcher loaded with inert drill rounds for handling/loading training by ground crew.

The M261 was developed at the same time as the M260 rocket pod and is similar in construction, but with an increased diameter to accommodate nineteen 2.75in (70mm) rockets. They are in service with the US Army for use with the Hydra 70 rockets on their AH-1 Cobra and AH-64 Apache attack helicopters. In 1996 the M261 was selected by the British Army for use with their WAH-64 Longbow Apaches and these will be armed with the CRV7 rockets.

TYPE:	80MM S-8 ROCKET

Manufacturer:	Vympel
Country of manufacture:	Russia
Diameter:	3.15in (80mm)
Length:	4.9ft to 5.6ft (1.5 to 1.7m)
Weight:	Up to 33.5lb (15.2kg)

The Vympel-designed and built 80mm S-8 rocket is thought to have evolved during the late 1970s with four specific warheads – HEAT, penetration, fuel air explosive and illumination, although a chaff and anti-tank variants followed later. Two twenty-round launch pods were designed to accommodate the S-8 – the B-8V20A with an open front carried on helicopters and the B-8M1 with a conical nose for use by fixed-wing aircraft.

The S-8 rocket is in service with Russian and most former Warsaw Pact air forces including Czech, Hungary and Poland.

ABOVE: The helicopter variant B-8V20A seen here mounted on a Mi-35 can accommodate twenty of the S-8 rockets, of which one is protruding.

BELOW: The B-8M1 is aerodynamically streamlined for use by fixed-wing aircraft.

80mm S-8M rockets.

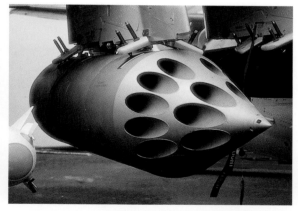

TYPE:	81MM MEDUSA ROCKET LAUNCHER SYSTEM

Manufacturer:	SNIA BPD
Country of manufacture:	Italy
Diameter:	15.59in (396mm)
Length:	7.55ft (2.3m)

The SNIA 81mm Medusa rocket system comprises a family of 51mm (2in), 81mm (3in) and 122mm (4.8in) rockets designed for use by helicopters and aircraft. During the 1980s, these unguided rockets were incorporated into a modular system which enabled the rocket launcher to interface with the aircraft weapon system so as to take advantage of laser range finding and provide detail in head-up displays to improve weapon delivery. At the same time, the range of rockets was extended, including one to deal with armour.

The Medusa rocket launchers are built in three sizes – six-, seven- and twelve-tube capacity. The seven-tube launcher is purely for helicopter use, while the others are available in two types – HAL for helicopter/subsonic air-

craft and SAL for supersonic aircraft. The dimensions given are for the 81-HAL-12. The weight depends on the rockets fitted.

The 81mm Medusa system together with the 51mm and 122mm rocket are understood to be in service with the Italian armed forces.

LEFT: The SNIA BPD 81mm 81-HAL-12 rocket launcher pod mounted on a WS.70 Black Hawk.

TYPE:	100MM MULTI-DART 100 ROCKET

Manufacturer:	TDA (Thomson Brandt)
Country of manufacture:	France
Diameter:	3.94in (100mm)
Length:	9.02ft (2.75m)

Thomson Brandt began development of the 100mm Multi-Dart 100 at the same time as their Multi-Dart 68 rockets. These rockets are comprised of a number of high-velocity darts that were capable of piercing armour. While the original 100mm (3.94in) rockets could be carried by either helicopters or aircraft, the Multi-Dart 100 requires a high kinetic energy to penetrate the armour. As a result, they are less effective when fired from helicopters and are only usually carried by aircraft.

Three variants of the Multi-Dart 100 rocket have been developed for use against different targets. The Type AB warhead is fitted with six

1.65kg (3.6lb) darts which can penetrate 80mm (3in) of armour plate. The ABL has thirty-six 190g (0.4lb) darts for use against up to 15mm (0.6in) of armour plate and the AMV has 192 35g (0.07lb) darts for use against up to 8mm (0.3in) of armour.

The Multi-Dart 100 has been cleared for use with several aircraft including the Alpha Jet, Jaguar, Mirage F.1 and 2000 and Super Etendard, and is currently in use with the French, German, Greek and Portuguese Air Forces.

A pair of 100mm Multi-Dart rockets together with an LR.FR or 100-4 launcher pod. Also in the photo at the rear are the LR.68.12 and LR.68.22 for 68mm rockets. Next to them is an AEREA HL-10-70 for 70mm rockets. Next to the Bell 412 is a triple SNIA 122mm HL-3-122 launcher with rocket, and above is the 81mm 81-HLA-12, also built by SNIA.

Manufacturer:	Vympel
Country of manufacture:	Russia
Diameter:	4.8in (122mm)
Length:	9.81ft (2.99m)
Weight:	165lb (75kg)

122mm S-13T rockets together with a B-13L launcher pod.

The 122mm S-13 rocket was developed on the late 1970s as an air-to-ground rocket capable of penetrating concrete structures such as buildings and runways. Further development added anti-armour, fragmentation and fuel air explosive variants.

The S-13 rocket can be launched from either fixed-wing or helicopters using the B-13L rocket pod. This five-round pod is similar in construction for both fixed-wing and helicopters, although the latter dispenses with the conical nose, reducing its length to 3.06m (10ft) and is designated B-13L-1. The data is for the anti-armour S-13T which has a tandem warhead.

The B-13L can be fitted to most Russian attack aircraft and is in use with Russian and most of the former Warsaw Pact air forces including those of the Czech Republic, Hungary and Poland.

Manufacturer:	AEREA
Country of manufacture:	Italy
Diameter:	16.61in (422mm)
Length:	5.05ft (1.54m)
Weight:	Up to 551lb (250kg)

The Aerea range of rocket launcher pods can be fitted to most NATO aircraft fitted with standard weapon lugs, and are widely used by the Italian armed forces as well as a number of others.

The AEREA HL-19-70 launcher pod accommodates nineteen 70mm rockets and is designed for use with helicopters.

Aerea developed a range of rocket pods that could be fitted to standard NATO mounting points. These pods are compatible with fast jet attack aircraft, training aircraft or helicopters and come in a range of calibres. A protective nose fairing is usually fitted on the nose when carried by the faster aircraft, which also improves the pod's aerodynamic properties. It is of a frangible construction, allowing the rockets to fire through it without interference to the rocket performance.

The designation of the pod indicates the type of carrier (for example, AL = Aircraft Launched, HL = Helicopter Launched and SAL = Supersonic Aircraft Launched), followed by number of tubes. The number of tubes depends on the mission and the rocket warhead and can vary from four or six for training, target marking or the larger calibre, through to twenty-nine for area attack. This last number of the designation indicates the calibre. These are 50 for the 2in (51mm), 70 for the 2.75in (70mm), 80 for the 81mm and 122 for the 122mm. The data supplied is for an HL-19-70 –Helicopter Launched, nineteen-tube and 70mm calibre. So far, Aerea have produced eighteen rocket launcher pods.

TYPE: BRD Training Bomb and Rocket Launcher Pod

Manufacturer:	AEREA
Country of manufacture:	Italy
Diameter:	16.97in (431mm)
Length:	7.87ft (2.4m)
Weight:	353lb approx (160kg)

The Aerea family of BRD rocket pods were designed to be used with various rocket calibres and practice bombs for use with fixed-wing aircraft of the Italian Air Force.

The designations have been constructed to indicate the number of practice bombs carried, followed by the number of rockets, followed by their calibre. For example, Bomb and Rocket Dispenser BRD-4-250 is the carrier for four practice bombs plus two 50mm (2in) rockets and is also available for 68 (2.65in) and 70mm (2.73in) calibres, while the BRD-4-4CRV7 almost follows the rule in that the four rockets are named as the CRV7. The 68 and 70mm are also available for four rockets. The total weight of the pod is dependent on the warheads fitted.

LEFT: An inverted BRD-4-2CRV showing the bomb racks, together with a pair of Mk.76 and 106 practice bombs and a CRV-7 rocket.

BELOW: The BRD-4-250 and others in this range are used for training purposes only.

TYPE: HMP and RMP Pod Weapon System

Manufacturer:	FN Herstal
Country of manufacture:	Belgium
Diameter:	16.1in (410mm)
Length:	5ft 11.3in (1.81m)
Height:	18.1in (0.46m)
Weight:	394.7lb (180kg)

The HMP and RMP (Heavy Machine-gun Pod and Rocket Machine-gun Pod) were developed in the 1970s to provide helicopters that would normally be unarmed with a self-defence or even a light attack capability.

The HMP was developed by FN Herstal in the 1970s as a bolt-on system. Further development in the 1980s combined the 12.7mm (0.5in) gun with four tubes capable of firing most standard 70mm (2.75in) rockets and was designated HMP-RL. A similar RMP pod was also built which used lighter materials but only carried three rockets and was designed for lighter helicopter. The HMP-RL is more suited to the multi-role helicopter or subsonic aircraft.

The HMP-RL combined gun and rocket pod. Also displayed next to the AS656 Panther is the TBA (now TDA) LR-68-22 and the FN Herstal LAU-19A rocket launcher pods.

Manufacturer:	**FN Herstal**
Country of manufacture:	**Belgium**
Diameter:	**10.4in (265mm)**
Length:	**6ft 2.8in (1.90m)**
Weight:	**273lb approx (124kg max)**

In addition to producing rockets, FN Herstal make a range of rocket launcher pods. These can accommodate not only their own rockets but virtually any other 2.75in (70mm) diameter rockets of the FFAR (Folding Fin Air Rocket) or the Wrap Around design.

The LAU-7A rocket launcher pod (data provided) has seven tubes with a dual-purpose trigger. It is an easy system to load and can be fitted to any aircraft equipped to accept rocket launchers. The nose section is streamlined for aerodynamic efficiency on fixed-wing aircraft. The life of the tubes in the LAU-7A is in excess of 100 firings, after which they can be replaced. Others in the range include the LAU-19A, which accommodates nineteen rockets and also has the aerodynamic nose

for use with aircraft. The LAU-7H, LAU-12H and LAU-19H have seven, twelve or nineteen rockets respectively, have a flat nose and are for use on helicopters.

The LAU-7A rocket launcher pod is stressed for use on fixed-wing aircraft.

9M17 SKORPION (AT-2 'SWATTER') MISSILE

Manufacturer:	Nudelman
Country of manufacture:	Russia
Diameter:	5.2in (132mm)
Span:	2.17m (660mm)
Length:	3.81m (1.16m)
Weight:	65lb (29.4kg)

The 9M17 Skorpion anti-tank missile began development in the 1960s for ground and air launch. It was allocated the NATO reporting designation of AT-2 'Swatter'.

The 9M17 Skorpion has been built in large numbers. Development over the years is believed to have led to wire, radio and infrared seeker guidance variants.

The Skorpion has seen wide service carried by Mi-8/17 and Mi-24 helicopters. It was used by the Russian and former Warsaw Pact armed forces and may still be in service with some.

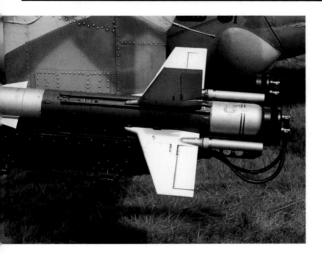

The 9M17 Skorpion anti-tank missile on a Mi-24. (Photo Paul Jackson)

TYPE: 9M14 MALYUTKA (AT-3 'SAGGER') MISSILE

Manufacturer:	Kolomna
Country of manufacture:	Russia
Diameter:	4.92in (125mm)
Span:	15.35in (390mm)
Length:	3.22ft (980mm)
Weight:	27.56lb (12.5kg)
Range:	1.9 miles (3km)

The 9M14 Malyutka anti-tank missile was originally developed as a ground-launched anti-tank missile in the late 1950s and was allocated the NATO reporting designation of AT-3 'Sagger'. This wire-guided missile has since migrated to form an effective weapon for use from helicopters.

ABOVE: Three 9M14 Malyutka mounted on a Mi-17.

RIGHT: Captured ex-Iraqi 9M14s awaiting destruction by the Allied forces in Kuwait.

The several models of the 9M14 Malyutka have been built. The early were fitted with a conical nose and varied in length from 860mm (33.5in) to 900mm (35in). Later models featured a tandem warhead, enabling them to attack tanks with reactive armour. These are recognized by the elongated thin nose.

TYPE:	9M114 KOKON (AT-6/AT-9 'SPIRAL') MISSILE

Manufacturer:	Kolomna
Country of manufacture:	Russia
Diameter:	5.12in (130mm)
Length:	5.74m (1.75m)
Weight:	85lb (38.5kg)
Range:	3.7 miles (6km)

The 9M114 anti-tank missile was developed during the 1970s and first appeared in the early 1980s. It was allocated the NATO reporting designation AT-6 'Spiral'. This tube-mounted missile is primarily for use against ground targets such as tanks and vehicles. It also has a limited air-to air capability against airborne helicopters. The 9M114 is also available as a ground-launched missile.

The 9M114 Kokon is stored in a sealed tube containing a single missile. The tube is 1.98m (6.5ft) long and 370mm (14.4in) in diameter and acts as the launcher. It is believed that the missile is then controlled in flight by a radio link. It can be fitted with a HEAT or fragmentation warhead. The AT-9 has an improved data link, warhead and range.

The AT-6/AT-9 missiles can be operated from a number of helicopters including the Mi-8 and Mi-24. Various launcher arrangements permit up to sixteen missiles to be carried on the Mi-28 and Mi-35. The 9M114 is in use with a number of operators of these helicopters including the Czech Republic, Hungary and Poland.

Two quad launchers of the 9M114 Kokon on a Mi-35 with a B-8V-20 rocket launcher pod.

TYPE: 3KG AND 14KG PRACTICE BOMBS

Manufacturer:	Portsmouth Aviation
Country of manufacture:	UK
Diameter:	3in (76mm)
Span:	6.3in (153mm)
Length:	15in (381mm)
Weight:	7.2lb (3.3kg)

Portsmouth Aviation designed and produce the 3kg and 14kg practice bombs for the British MoD.

Two sizes of practice bomb are currently used – the 3kg which is used to replicate retarded bombs and the 14kg for the Mk.80 series of bombs. On impact with the ground they eject a jet of smoke to aid spotting. Drag plates can be fitted to the 3kg practice bomb to give adjustment to replicate specific bombs.

Both the 3kg and the 14kg practice bombs currently serve with the RAF and are fitted into the CBLS pods, which can be fitted to most

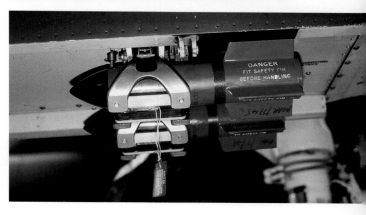

3kg practice bombs in a CBLS.

training and attack aircraft including the Alpha Jet, Hawk, Jaguar and Tornado. A number of them have been exported.

TYPE: 500LB GP BOMBS (MK.1/2)

Manufacturer:	BAE Systems (Royal Ordnance)
Country of manufacture:	UK
Diameter:	13in (330mm)
Span:	18.1 (460mm)
Length:	6.56m (2m)
Weight:	573lb (260kg)

The 500lb General Purpose (GP) bombs used by the RAF were developed by Royal Ordnance from bombs used during World War II. They have seen improvements to enable their continued use by fast jet aircraft

One of the improvements to the 250lb bomb has been to modify their shape slightly to make them more streamlined; however, the main improvements have been internally with the fuzes and explosive charge. There is a Mk.1 and Mk.2, which have two different explosive fillings, and there is a small difference in weight. Two types of tail can be fitted to these bombs – the No. 116 standard ballistic or the No. 118 Retarded.

The 500lb GP bomb is cleared for use with the Harrier, Hawk, Jaguar Sea Harrier and Tornado and is used by the RAF and the Royal Navy.

A 500lb GP bomb on an RAF Jaguar, together with an AIM-9L Sidewinder missile and a Phimat pod.

TYPE: 1,000LB GP BOMBS (MK.10, MK.13, MK.18, MK.20, MK.22)

Manufacturer:	BAE Systems (Royal Ordnance)
Country of manufacture:	UK
Diameter:	16.54in (420mm)
Span:	1.9ft (580mm)
Length:	7.41ft (2.26m)
Weight:	Up to 948lb (430kg)

The 1,000lb General Purpose (GP) bombs used by the RAF were originally a development by Royal Ordnance of the bomb design of World War II. However, they have seen improvements to enable their continued use by fast jet aircraft.

The 1,000lb GP bomb has currently reached Mk.22 and stocks of a number continue to serve in various roles. As with the 500lb GP, most of the improvements are internal such as fuzes and explosive. Three types of tail can be fitted – the No. 107 and the 114, which are the standard ballistic type, and the No. 117 retarded tail. Kits have been produced to enable the Paveway II and III to be fitted.

A 1,000lb GP inert training bomb on the centre pylon of an RAF Tornado GR.1.

TYPE:	RETARDER TYPE 117 AND 118

Manufacturer: Portsmouth Aviation/Hunting Engineering
Country of manufacture: UK

The Retarder Type 117 and 118 comprise a tail unit which can be bolted onto the 1,000lb and 500lb bombs to enable them to be dropped at low level and allow the aircraft to depart before the bombs explode.

The Type 117 and 118 appear similar but are designed to fit the 1,000lb and 500lb respectively. On being dropped from the aircraft the bomb clears that aircraft and then a timer releases the retarder arms. These are basically formed from the outer skin of the tail section which splits into four sections and is hinged at the rear of the tail. Attached to these arms and making a disc is a ribbon parachute. This sequence is linked to the arming of the bomb so that should the retarder fail to open, the bomb will not be armed and will not pose a threat to the aircraft.

The Retarder can be fitted to any of the 500lb and 1,000lb in live and practice bombs used by the RAF and Royal Navy and can be used by any aircraft capable of carrying these bombs. These include the Harrier, Hawk, Jaguar, Sea Harrier and Tornado. Adapters have been produced to enable the Retarder to be fitted to the Mk.80 series of bombs. It is believed that the Retarder has been exported to several other air arms.

A 500lb (nearest) and a 1,000lb inert training bomb with the Type 118 and Type 117 Retarder tails.

A Type 117 Retarder tail unit deployed showing the arms spread.

TYPE:	ADM-141 TALD/ITALD DECOY MISSILE

Manufacturer:	IMI/Brunswick
Country of manufacture:	Israel
Span:	5.09ft (1.55m)
Length:	7ft 8in (2.34m)
Weight:	401lb (182kg)
Max speed:	Mach 0.8
Range:	184 miles (297km)
Ceiling:	30,000ft (9,144m)

Not strictly a weapon, the ITALD is a development of the TALD (Tactical Air-Launched Decoy) which is carried by aircraft to enhance their SEAD role and also to make their mission safer.

ITALD is a stand-off air-launched decoy which was designed by IMI with a radar repeater that produces a return resembling that of an attacking aircraft. Launched to stimulate enemy SAM sites, it then saturates the enemy radar, making it possible for anti-radiation missiles such as HARM to be launched at the sites with less risk.

TALD was built by IMI for the Israeli Air Force, and by Brunswick for the US Navy as the ADM-141. In the early 1990s Brunswick developed an improved TALD referred to as ITALD and designated ADM-141. Of similar size, ITALD features a turbojet which increases the range to 160nm. ITALD can be pre-programmed to fly realistic flight profiles with speeds from Mach 0.45 to Mach 0.8 and at heights from 500ft (152m) to 30,000ft (9,144m). Its onboard navigation and GPS system enables it to fly over a number of way points as well as terrain following, giving it a fire-and-forget capability. The ITALD can be fitted to a standard bomb rack, enabling carriage by a number of aircraft types.

The ADM-141C ITALD decoy with its wings deployed.

All production of the ITALD is currently undertaken by IMI, with deliveries to the USN as well as the Israeli Air Force for use on F/A-18, F-4, F-16 and S-3 aircraft.

TYPE:	AGM-45 SHRIKE MISSILE

Manufacturer:	Raytheon (Texas Instruments)
Country of manufacture:	USA
Diameter:	8in (203mm)
Span:	3ft (914mm)
Length:	10ft (3.05)
Weight:	390lb (177kg)
Max speed:	Mach 2
Range:	25 miles (40km)

The AGM-45 Shrike was developed as an anti-radiation missile in the early 1960s at the Naval Weapons Center at China Lake. In 1963 Texas Instruments headed a consortium to build the missile, which entered service in 1965.

The AGM-45 Shrike was based on the AGM-7 Sparrow airframe and uses a passive radar sensor to detect and target the transmission source. With the sensor only able to detect a relatively narrow band of radiated signal frequencies, series of new heads were constantly being designed to meet new threats as they were detected. Shrike was first used operationally in Vietnam with limited success and was also used in the Gulf War. During this period at least a dozen different heads were built.

An AGM-45 Shrike under the wing of an F-16 Fighting Falcon.

The AGM-45 Shrike was used with the Wild Weasel F-105 and EA-6 in Vietnam and later was cleared on A-4, A-7, F-4, EF-111 and Vulcan. Apart from use by the US Air Force and Navy, Shrike was exported to a number of countries around the world including Belgium, Denmark, Greece, Norway, Turkey and the UK. Shrike has been superseded by the Alarm and HARM, but a few of the many thousand built may still remain on the inventory of one to two air forces.

TYPE:	AGM-65 MAVERICK MISSILE

Manufacturer:	Raytheon (Hughes)
Country of manufacture:	USA
Diameter:	12in (305mm)
Span:	2ft 4in (720mm)
Length:	8ft 2in (2.49m)
Weight:	Up to 677lb (307kg)
Range:	Up to 15.5 miles (25km)

Hughes commenced development of the AGM-65 Maverick in the mid 1960s as a TV-guided missile. It entered service in 1972. This highly successful weapon has proved to be simple to use and effective against tanks and other ground targets. With a relatively low cost, its production has been substantial. As

An inert AGM-65 Maverick with the scene-magnification head still enabled allows the pilot to practice using the missile seeker to search for the target.

The RAF is a recent customer for the Maverick and an AGM-65G-2 can be seen on a Harrier GR.7, together with an LAU5003 rocket launcher pod for the CRV7.

well as meeting USAF requirements, the USMC and US Navy have ordered substantial quantities or variants which have capabilities that are more effective against ships. Several warheads and fuzes can be used on the Maverick and these are interchangeable.

A number of Maverick models have been built, commencing with the AGM-65, which was the basic TV model. The AGM-65B featured improved optics to magnify the image as well as other minor improvements. The AGM-65C featured a laser guidance with designation either from another aircraft or from the ground. The AGM-65D featured an IR seeker that enabled lock-on to targets at twice the range of previous models and could be used in bad weather or at night. The AGM-65E was a development of the C especially for the USMC with a more effective blast/fragmentation warhead and digital processing. The AGM-65F is a Navy version of the D with the more effective blast/fragmention warhead. The AGM-65G has an IR seeker but with modified software to enable spot designation of larger targets. The AGM-65H

is similar to the A/B model, but with an improved picture and lighter construction. The AGM-65J is a similar model for the USMC, but with the effective blast/fragmentation warhead. The AGM-65K is similar to the J with the larger warhead but with minor modifications for the USAF.

The AGM-65 Maverick has been cleared for use with a wide range of aircraft including A-7, A-10, AV-8B, F-4, F-5, F-15, F-16 F/A-18 and the Gripen as well as the P-3. It can also be used on helicopters such as the AH-1W and SH-2G. The RAF have recently added the AGM-65G Maverick to their inventory for use on the Harrier GR.7. The Maverick has proved popular with many armed forces and is in use with twenty-four countries throughout the world and over 30,000 have been built. Other NATO users include Belgium, Denmark, Germany, Italy, Netherlands, Norway, Portugal, Spain and Turkey.

It was reported that some 5,300 Maverick missiles were fired during the Gulf War and 4,800 claimed successful strikes on tanks, vehicles, pieces of artillery and other targets.

TYPE:	AGM-86 ALCM/CALCM CRUISE MISSILE

Manufacturer:	Boeing
Country of manufacture:	USA
Diameter:	27.28in (693mm)
Span:	12ft (3.65m)
Length:	20ft 9in (6.32m)
Weight:	3,214lb (1,458kg)
Range:	1,550 miles (2,500km)

The development of the AGM-86 Air-Launched Cruise Missile (ALCM) commenced during the mid 1970s, although there had been proposals before that. The AGM-86 was designed to accommodate either a nuclear or conventional warhead and be carried by the B-52H.

Four models of the AGM-86 have been built. The AGM-86A was the prototype, but it did not

An AGM-86 during a test flight. (Photo Boeing via API)

Here, 322 nuclear-armed AGM-86B are being converted to the conventional-armed AGM-86C CALCM. (Photo Boeing via API)

A substantial number of the AGM-86C were launched from B-52s at Serb targets in the former Yugoslavia and at Iraqi targets. (Photo Boeing via API)

enter production. It was 2m shorter than the subsequent production missiles. 1,715 AGM-86Bs were built, armed with the W-80 nuclear warhead. They were designed to be launched in substantial numbers to saturate defences and enable manned aircraft to have safer penetration to major targets. The AGM-86C is a converted AGM-86B with a new engine and a conventional warhead. Also known as the Conventional Air-Launched Cruise Missile or CALCM, this model was first used operationally during the Gulf War and again during operations against Serb targets. Boeing is currently converting of 322 nuclear AGM-86B to CALCM for the USAF. The last fifty of the ALCMs being converted will be to AGM-86D standard with a penetration warhead.

TYPE:	AGM-88 HARM MISSILE

Manufacturer:	Raytheon (Texas)
Country of manufacture:	USA
Diameter:	10in (254mm)
Span:	3ft 8.5in (1.13m)
Length:	13ft 8.5in (4.18m)
Weight:	807lb (366kg)
Max speed:	Mach 2+
Range:	11.5 miles (18.5km)

The AGM-88 HARM High-speed Anti Radiation Missile was developed by Texas Instruments in the late 1970s and has largely superseded the earlier AGM-45 Shrike and AGM-78 Standard missiles. The AGM-88 was first flown in 1979 and entered operational service with the USAF in 1983.

A USAF ground crew checks an AGM-88 HARM on a 52nd FW F-16CJ Fighting Falcon at Aviano, Italy, prior to a mission over the former Yugoslavia.

The HARM has three modes of operation. Self-protect is where the aircraft sensors have detected a radar emission; this will be classified by the computer and prioritized depending on threat level. This information is then indicated to the pilot and fed to the missile. The whole operation takes place in a fraction of a second, making the missile available for firing on the pilot's command. In the pre-briefed role, a radar signature or signatures are allocated to the sensor before the missile is launched towards a known threat area. The missile travels at around Mach 7 towards the target using INS navigation and around 7 to 10 miles (11–16km) from the target the seeker is activated. Should the designated radar have been switched off, the missile will then seek an alternative transmission to target or self-destruct.

In the SEAD role the missile seeker is switched on to detect any enemy radar transmissions and used together to enhance the aircraft's own sensors to scan and locate any threat transmissions before being fired.

There are four basic HARM models, although a number of sub-variants emerged as development progressed. The AGM-88A requires the search parameters to be changed at Depot level, while the AGM-88B, which was introduced in the late 1980s, can have the software reloaded on the flight-line. Many are being upgraded with the seeker of the C model. The AGM-88C has improved avionics, seeker and warhead, while the

AGM-88D has an additional GPS navigation to enable it to continue to a target even though the radar may be switched off. To confuse matters, the NATO-operated HARM designations are different to those used by the USAF and Navy, in that most missiles are designated AGM-88B with Block No. variants

The introduction of the ASQ-213 HARM Targeting System (HTS) pod enabled a improved targeting mode that included a long-range capability where the range could be calculated by the HTS and supplied to the missile system so that it could operate in its most effective mode. The ASQ-213 pod is mounted on the port side of the air intake of an F-16CJ in the same position as the LANTIRN pod fitted to some other F-16 variant, but is about half the size.

The HARM missiles were widely used during the Gulf War and in operations over the former Yugoslavia. They were carried by A-6 Intruder, A-7 Corsair and Wild Weasel F-4G Phantom. They are currently carried mainly by the EA-6B Prowler, F-16 Fighting Falcon, F/A-18 Hornet and Tornado IDS/ECR aircraft.

TYPE:	AGM-114 HELLFIRE MISSILE

Manufacturer:	Boeing (Rockwell)
Country of manufacture:	USA
Diameter:	7in (178mm)
Span:	13in (330mm)
Length:	5ft 4in (1.63m)
Weight:	99–110lb (45–50kg)
Max speed:	Mach 1.17
Range:	5 miles (8km)

The AGM-114 Hellfire (Heliborne, Laser, Fire and Forget) missile was designed in the 1970s by Rockwell as a modular-system, anti-armour weapon with a capability for precision attacks against bunkers and other valuable structures. The specification required that the missile would be effective against moving as well as stationary targets.

The first guided launch of Hellfire was from an AH-1G Cobra in 1978 and following successful trials. It entered service with the US Army in 1985 as the AGM-114A. Development progressed to the AGM-114B for the US Navy with a reduced smoke motor, as well as an arming device to increase safety aboard ships. The US Army also ordered an AGM-114B without the arming device, designated AGM-114C. The next production model was the AGM-114F, which had the ability to defeat reactive armour by using a small initial charge to set it off. The length was increased to 1.8m (5.9ft) to accommodate the extra warhead.

The AGM-114K was developed after the Gulf War to rectify some deficiencies that the conflict identified with this successful missile, together with some already programmed improvements. This included resolving the poor acquisition of targets designated by laser but partially obscured by smoke. In addition, there were various improvements to the warhead and seeker, as well as countermeasure distraction. With all of these capability enhancements this model became known as the Hellfire 2. A variant with added safety features and a blast/fragmentation warhead was ordered by the US Navy as the AGM-114M for use on their AH-1W Super Cobras.

Development continued with the AGM-114L variant which uses millimetric-wave in place of the laser seeker, enabling a day/night/all-weather capability for use with the AH-64D Longbow Apache. In the UK, a variant named Brimstone (see separate entry) was developed and has been ordered for the British Army for use on fast jets as well as helicopters.

Two helicopter launchers are used for Hellfire – the M272 was the initial model, but this has been superseded by the M299 which has a full digital interface for the later missile variants. Both models are available in two or four launch rail configurations.

In addition to the air-launched missile, variants of Hellfire have been developed for coastal defence and fitting to a number of vehicles for surface-to-surface use. An air-to-air variant has been investigated.

Extensive use was made of Hellfire during the Gulf War, with an estimated 4,000 missiles being fired at Iraqi targets. In February 2001 an interesting and logical development of the use of Hellfire was when one was launched from an RQ-1A Predator. This Unmanned Air Vehicle (UAV) was designed and used for the reconnaissance role; in attempts to reduce aircrew casualties this

Inert AGM-114 Hellfire missiles on a US Army AH-64A Apache plus an M261 rocket launcher pod.

has to be the ultimate and the beginning of the real Star Wars scenario. Already, the larger Predator B has been quoted as capable of carrying up to sixteen Hellfire missiles.

The AGM-114 Hellfire is used by the US Army on their AH-1, AH-64, OH-58 and UH-60 and will be carried on the RAH-66. It can be used by the US Navy and USMC on their SH-60 and AH-1W. Exports have been made to a number of countries throughout the world and include Canada, Greece, the Netherlands, Turkey and the UK as well as a number of other non-NATO countries.

TYPE: AGM-122 SIDEARM MISSILE

Manufacturer:	NAWC/Motorola
Country of manufacture:	USA
Diameter:	5in (127mm)
Span:	2ft 1in (0.63m)
Length:	10ft (3.05m)
Weight:	200lb (91kg)
Max speed:	Mach 2.5
Range:	11 miles (18km)

The AGM-122 Sidearm is converted from surplus AIM-9C for the US Navy and USMC.

The AGM-122A Sidearm (SIDEwinder Anti-Radiation Missile) is a rebuilt surplus AIM-9C using a passive semi-active radar seeker. It is designed by China Lake Naval Weapons Center and built by Motorola. Modifications were carried out in the mid 1980s to provide a cheap but effective anti-radiation missile for the USMC and US Navy for use on their A-4, AV-8A/B, F/A-18, as well as the AH-1T helicopters. Although not as sophisticated as the AGM-88 HARM missile and open to distraction by countermeasures, the AGM-122A Sidearm achieved its objective with around 1,000 missiles refurbished and modified.

Plans for an improved model with a new seeker were proposed and designated as the AGM-122B, but this has been superseded by the AARGM (see separate entry).

TYPE: AGM-129 ACM MISSILE

Manufacturer:	Raytheon (General Dynamics)
Country of manufacture:	USA
Diameter:	27in (686mm)
Span:	10ft 2in (3.1m)
Length:	20ft 10in (6.35m)
Weight:	3,709lb (1,684kg)
Range:	1,865 miles (3,000km)

General Dynamic commenced development of the AGM-129 Advanced Cruise Missile (ACM) in 1983 as a replacement for the AGM-86 ALCM. First flown in July 1985, the ACM features stealth technology and it has a longer range than the

The Boeing AGM-129 ACM. (Photo Boeing via API)

ALCM. It is armed with a W80 nuclear warhead and has a powerful navigation system which can evade enemy ground- and air-based defences. It can attack heavily defended targets with great precision using a laser radar during the terminal sequence. In November 1987 McDonnell Douglas became the second-source contractor and a total of 461 were built.

The AGM-129A entered service with the USAF in June 1990 and was designed to be carried by the B-1B, B-2A and B-52H, although it is reported that it will only be carried by forty-eight of the B-52s based at Barksdale and Minot AFBs. The missiles can be carried internally on a rotary launcher or on pylons under the wing.

Variants include the AGM-129B which was to be armed with either a conventional warhead or submunitions; however, this did not enter production. The AGM-129C is a USAF proposal for a modified AGM-129A which would incorporate GPS and a conventional penetration warhead.

TYPE:	AGM-130 MISSILE

Manufacturer:	Boeing (McDonnell Douglas)
Country of manufacture:	USA
Diameter:	18in (457mm)
Span:	4ft 11in (1.5m)
Length:	12ft 10in (3.91m)
Weight:	2,917lb (1,324kg)
Range:	40 miles (64km)

Rockwell began development of the AGM-130 air-to-surface missile in the early 1980s. It made its first flight in 1984, and was produced to meet a USAF requirement for a product improvement over the GBU-15 but at a lower cost.

The AGM-130 is similar to the GBU-15, but is fitted with a rocket motor to give it double the stand-off range. Like the GBU-15, it utilizes the 2,000lb Mk.84 bomb, although it can also use the BLU-109 with a penetrating warhead. The guidance system uses either TV or IR and the images are transmitted by data link back to the Weapons Systems Operator (WSO), who can monitor the weapon and give corrections if required. The AGM-130 can fly autonomously using INS/GPS or can be flown on to the target manually.

Several models of the AGM-130 have been proposed, with production commencing with the AGM-130 with the 2,000lb Mk.84 GP bomb as the warhead. The AGM-130B utilizes the SUU-54 dispenser as the warhead. Also built is the AGM-

An inert USAF AGM-130 used for ground training.

130C, which uses the BLU-109 penetration warhead. Further proposals replace the rocket motor with a turbojet and incorporate target recognition and laser seekers.

Initial deliveries were made to the USAF in 1992 with a requirement for 600 weapons. This was a reduction from the original planned requirement of around 4,000, but following their successful use in the Gulf War and against Serb targets in Kosovo this may well be increased.

TYPE:	AGM-142 HAVE NAP (POPEYE 1) MISSILE

Manufacturer:	Rafael
Country of manufacture:	Israel
Diameter:	21in (533mm)
Span:	5ft 8in (1.73m)
Length:	15ft 10in (4.83m)
Weight:	3,000lb (1,362kg)
Range:	62 miles (100km)

The Rafael AGM-142 Have Nap is an advanced, precision-guided, air-to-ground missile derived from the Popeye missile that is in service with Israeli Air Force tactical aircraft. It is designed to be effective against high-value ground and sea targets such as power plants, missile sites, bridges, ships and bunkers. It features a multiple guidance mode and options provide high accuracy, allowing targeting at a building doorway. The AGM-142 can be launched at significant stand-off ranges from the target. It is currently used by the USAF with the B-52H bomber; however, the missile is adaptable to a variety of aircraft.

A USAF B-52H Stratofortress taxies out for a mission against Serb targets with three of its load of four AGM-142 Have Nap missiles visible.

The AGM-142 entered production in 1989. It employs mid-course autonomous guidance based on inertial navigation, then homes in on the target using a high-performance IIR or TV seeker. These are interchangeable and can be changed prior to the mission. The missile guides automatically to the selected target. It is armed with either a 1,000lb blast/fragmentation or penetrating warhead.

Four variants of the AGM-142 have been built. The AGM-142A is fitted with a TV seeker and a 750lb blast/fragmentation warhead. The AGM-142B has an IIR seeker and the same warhead. The AGM-142C has a TV seeker with an 800lb penetrator bomb, while the AGM-142D has the IIR seeker with the same penetrator bomb.

The AGM-142 saw limited unsuccessful use from B-52s for attacks against Serb targets during the Kosovo operations and following assessment they were withdrawn. It has been reported that subsequent modifications to their software has resolved the problem and that they remain in service.

In addition to being in service with the USAF, the AGM-142 Have Nap/Popeye is also in service with the Turkish Air Force. Outside NATO it is also in service with the Israeli Air Force, Republic of Korea Air Force and the RAAF.

TYPE: AGM-154 JSOW BOMB

Manufacturer:	Raytheon
Country of manufacture:	USA
Diameter:	13.4in (340mm)
Span:	8ft 10.3in (2.70m)
Length:	13ft 3in (4.06m)
Weight:	Up to 1,500lb (680kg)
Range:	Up to 37 miles (60km)

The AGM-154 is a modular weapon designed to accommodate a range of submunitions, seekers and tail units. It was planned as a low-cost common weapon for the US Navy and

The Raytheon AGM-154 Joint Stand-Off Weapon.

USAF and initially referred to as the Joint Stand-Off Weapon (JSOW).

Currently two models are in production for the USAF and US Navy. These are the AGM-154A, which carries 145 BLU-97 submunitions as carried by the CBU-87/B for use by the USAF, USMC and US Navy. The AGM-154B, with six BLU-108, is fitted in the CBU-97/B for the USAF and US Navy. Completing its trials for the US Navy is the AGM-154 which is armed with the BLU-111 submunition and a guidance computer using GPS/INS for navigation and IIR sensor for precision guidance on to the target.

A growth option is also envisaged to carry various combined-effects munitions, bomblets, mines, radar jammers and anti-armour, in addition to a 226–437kg (498lb–964lb) warhead. It could also be fitted with a small turbojet or rocket motor to increase its range as well as alternative seeker options.

The AGM-154 had been cleared on the F/A-18 and F-16 and will be carried by the AV-8B, B-1, B-2, B-52, F-15E, F-117 and P-3 on completion of carriage trials. It could also be carried by the Jaguar, Tornado and Typhoon.

Manufacturer:	Lockheed Martin
Country of manufacture:	USA
Span:	8ft 10in (2.7m)
Length:	14ft (4.27m)
Weight:	2,250lb (1,021.5kg)
Range:	115 miles+ (185km+)

The Joint Air-to-Surface Stand-off Missile (JASSM) is an autonomous, long-range, conventional, air-to-ground, precision stand-off cruise missile for the USAF and Navy. Designated AGM-158, it is designed to destroy high-value, well-defended, fixed and relocatable targets. JASSM's significant stand-off range helps to keep Air Force and Navy aircrews well out of danger from hostile air defence systems. The missile's mission effectiveness has been designed to provide a close to single-missile target kill capability.

The JASSM is navigated using INS/GPS and is fitted with a state-of-the-art infrared seeker to recognize the target which enables very accurate target acquisition and destruction. It is armed with a 1,000lb penetrator warhead and the stealthy airframe was designed to make it difficult to detect and destroy. It is also fitted with a data link, enabling it to transmit confirmation of its target acquisition.

During 1999 and 2000, a series of development JASSMs was successfully launched from F-16s. These

The AGM-158 JASSM missile with wings extended and tail folded and marked with silhouettes of aircraft with carriage clearance.

achieved their mission goals with a range of manoeuvring, including the Bomb Impact Assessment (BIA) transmission. Initial production was due to commence in 2001 and entry into service is scheduled for 2003.

Initial clearances for the JASSM have been made on the F-16 and B-52, but the B-1B, B-2, F-15E, F/A-18E/F and the F-117 will follow.

Manufacturer:	CMS/LFK
Country of manufacture:	Germany
Span:	24.8in (630mm)
Length:	11.38ft (3.47m)
Height:	12.6in (320mm)
Weight:	1,323lb approx (600kg)

The AFDS (Autonomous Free-flight Dispenser System) was developed by CMS of the USA from the LFK MW-1 Modular Dispenser System and

An AFDS dispenser is dropped by a USAF F-16 Fighting Falcon during trials. (Photo DASA via API)

DWS 24. The AFDS has been developed for use with the F-16, but can also be carried by the A-4, A-7, F-4 and F-5. Four of the AFDS can be carried by the F-16. Unlike the MW-1, which remains attached to the aircraft, the AFDS is released and can glide 10 to 20 km (6 to 12 miles), depending on the altitude from which it was dropped. As with the MW-1 and the DWS 24, the AFDS comprises three sections with an aerodynamic nose and finned tail section. The central body contains twenty-four tubes which can accommodate a range of submunitions according to the mission. These submunitions can include twenty-four tandem-charge RCBs for attacking runways, through to the smaller general purpose M42, of which nearly 2,000 can be fitted.

The AFDS has been ordered for the Greek Air Force for use with their A-7, F-4 and F-16s.

TYPE:	ALARM MISSILE

Manufacturer:	MBDA (BAe Dynamics)
Country of manufacture:	UK
Diameter:	8.7in (220mm)
Span:	2.36ft (720mm)
Length:	14.11ft (4.3m)
Weight:	584lb (265kg)
Range:	28 miles (45km)

An Alarm anti-radiation missile on a Gripen.

The development of the Alarm Anti-Radiation Missile (ARM) was begun by British Aerospace in the 1980s to meet an RAF requirement to replace their Shrike ARMs. Trials commenced in 1987 and deliveries commenced in 1991.

Alarm is a fire-and-forget missile – once enemy radar transmissions have been detected or are suspected, one or more missiles can be fired. It has five attack modes – all the pilot has to do is initialize firing while out of range of enemy anti-aircraft defence systems and the missile's pre-programmed mission will optimize the attack profile on the target radar. The missile is pre-programmed with a database of threat radars before take-off (these can be reprofiled during the flight if necessary) and then launched. It initially climbs to its operational height while flying to the area of the threat. At the same time, the onboard passive seeker searches for recognized threats and immediately one is detected, it dives to destroy the target. Should it arrive at the designated area and no threat be detected a parachute would be deployed and it would wait for a radar transmission. Once detected, the parachute would be jettisoned and the Alarm dive to attack the radar. For area suppression a ripple of missiles is launched and it is possible to create a safe corridor or area with onboard processors, ensuring that no more than one missile gets launched on to a single target. The universal mode provides an even greater stand-off range.

The nine Alarm missile can be carried by the Tornado GR.1/4/GR.4 and it will be cleared for used on the Typhoon. The Alarm is in service with the RAF and the only export is to Saudi Arabia.

TYPE:	APACHE/SCALP EG/STORM SHADOW DISPENSER MISSILE

Manufacturer:	MBDA (Matra BAe Dynamics)
Country of manufacture:	France/UK/Italy
Span:	9.84ft (3m)
Length:	16.73ft (5.10m)
Weight:	2,866lb (1,300kg)
Max speed:	621mph (1,000km/h)
Range:	155 miles (250km)

The Storm Shadow/SCALP EG (Emploi Général or general purpose) was developed from work conducted on the APACHE (Arme Propulsée A CHarges Ejectables) stand-off weapon to deliver submunitions. This French/German programme commenced in 1983, but was hit when the Germans decided to withdraw in 1988. However, France continued with the project. Several variants of APACHE were proposed, but when Matra merged with British Aerospace the project was developed to extend the range to give a cruise missile capability of 600km (373 miles).

The design gelled into Système de Croisière conventional Autonone à Longue Portée de precision (SCALP), which incorporates various navigation systems including inertial, digital terrain profiles and

ABOVE: *Apache on show at the Paris Air Show.*

In 1999 the Italians decided to join the programme, selecting the Storm Shadow for use on their Tornado and Typhoon, while the Greeks have ordered the SCALP EG for their Mirage 2000-5.

Initial production has commenced and the SCALP EG will be carried by French Air Force and Navy Mirage 2000D, 2000-5 and Rafale, while the Storm Shadow will be carried by the Tornado GR.4, Harrier GR.7 and Typhoon of the RAF.

BELOW: *Storm Shadow/SCALP EG.*

GPS. Designed to fly at low level, it has a passive IR imagery homing head, which is activated in the final phase of the attack to recognize the target and thus enable an extreme precision hit.

In the UK, Storm Shadow was developed in parallel and offered to the MoD to meet the SR (A) 1236 requirement for the RAF. This is the same weapon as the SCALP EG, but with some components and mission preparation systems designed for British rather than French operation.

The Storm Shadow/SCALP EG is a long-range cruise missile designed for attacks on strongly defended, armoured or high-value targets with an accurately recorded location.

TYPE:	ARMAT MISSILE

Manufacturer:	MBDA (Matra)
Country of manufacture:	France
Diameter:	15.75in (400mm)
Span:	3.94ft (1.2m)
Length:	13.52ft (4.15m)
Weight:	1,213lb (550kg)
Range:	Up to 55 miles (90km)

The ARMAT was developed from the AS 37 Martel and uses the same airframe. It entered service with the French Air Force in the mid 1980s as an anti-radar missile.

ARMAT features an improved passive radar homing sensor and several interchangeable models have been built to counter new threats. It has been cleared to be carried by the Atlantic, Jaguar, Mirage F.1 and Mirage 2000.

The ARMAT is currently in service with the French Air Force and several others in the Middle East.

A French Air Force banks revealing a pair of ARMAT anti-radar missiles plus a pair of R.550 Magic 2 air-to-air missiles. (Photo SIRPA Air/Matra via API)

Manufacturer:	MBDA (Aerospatiale)
Country of manufacture:	France
Diameter:	6.46in (164mm)
Span:	1.64ft (500mm)
Length:	3.97ft (1.21m)
Weight:	66lb (29.9kg)
Max speed:	360 mph (580km/h)
Range:	1.8 miles (3km)

The AS.11 airborne anti-tank missile was originally developed by Nord Aviation in the early 1950s from the ground-launched SS.11 anti-tank missile. It has seen many upgrades and improvements during the lengthy period that it served as a front-line missile. Early models required the operator to track the missile and fly it on to the target via controls transmitted to the missile through a fine wire. Later models simply required the operator to select the target and the system would automatically fly the missile to the designated spot.

A pair of AS.11s on a British Army Air Corps Scout. Although neither remain in British service, some may still serve in other countries.

The AS.11 can be armed with various warheads depending on the target, including fragmentation, semi-armour piercing, hollow-charged armour piercing, as well as a practice round.

The AS.11 has been carried by a number of helicopters including the Alouette II, Alouette III, Gazelle, Scout, Wasp and Wessex. Besides extensive operation by the French armed forces, they have been widely exported to various armed forces including those of Belgium, Germany, Greece, Italy, the Netherlands, the UK and the USA (operated as AGM-22A).

The AS.11 is now obsolete, but with production continuing until 1980 and around 180,000 missiles having been built, it is probable that some are still in service.

Manufacturer:	MBDA (Aerospatiale)
Country of manufacture:	France
Diameter:	8.27in (210mm)
Span:	2.13ft (650mm)
Length:	6.14ft (1.87m)
Weight:	167.5lb (76kg)
Range:	3 miles (5km)

Like the AS.11, the AS.12 has been overtaken by newer technology but may still be found in occasional use with a few of its many one-time operators.

AS.12 fitted on a Royal Navy Wasp. Both have been retired from RN service.

Development of the AS.12 air-to-ground missile was begun in the mid 1950s by Nord. Initially it was only planned to be a surface-to-surface missile, but its capabilities were soon recognized and this development of the AS.11 entered service in the early 1960s.

Armed with a visibly more powerful warhead than the AS.11 which was located in the bulbous nose section of the AS.12, its potential as an anti-ship missile was recognized by the French Navy and the Royal Navy. It was cleared for use on the Alize, Atlantic, Alouette, Gazelle, Neptune, Lynx, Nimrod, Wasp and Wessex.

Manufacturer:	MBDA (Aerospatiale)
Country of manufacture:	France
Diameter:	13.46in (342mm)
Span:	3.28ft (1m)
Length:	12ft (3.65m)
Weight:	1,146lb (520kg)
Range:	7.45 miles (12km)

The AS.30L air-to-ground missile is a development of the earlier AS.30, on which work began in the late 1950s. The AS.30L is a significant improvement over the AS.30, in that not only did the range improve from less than 3km (1.9 miles), but it also featured laser guidance to replace the radio link. The laser targeting can be via an aircraft-carried designator such the Atlis 2 pod or from a ground source.

ABOVE: An inert AS.30L air-to-ground missile fitted to a French Air Force Mirage 2000.

The AS.30L entered service in the mid 1980s with the French Air Force for use with their Jaguars and Navy Super Etendards. It was reported that some sixty missiles were fired by the French during the Gulf War.

RIGHT: An Atlis 2 laser-designator pod fitted to a Mirage 2000 and used to illuminate the target for the AS.30L and LGBs.

Manufacturer:	MBDA (Aerospatiale Matra)
Country of manufacture:	France
Diameter:	15in (380mm)
Span:	3.15ft (960mm)
Length:	17.65ft (5.38m)
Weight:	1,896lb (860kg)
Range:	155 miles (250km)

The ASMP (*Air-Sol Moyenne Portée* or medium-range air-to-surface) missile is a nuclear armed air-to-ground missile with a range of some 250km. It was the result of a competition between the proposed Matra turbojet-powered missile and the Aerospatiale ram-jet powered design. In 1978 the Aerospatiale design was selected and development commenced to replace the AN-22 nuclear bombs.

The supersonic ASMP became operational with the French Air Force in 1986, initially arming the Mirage IVP but since arming the Mirage 2000N and the Super Etendard of the French Navy.

ASMP navigation is by an inertial guidance system and incorporates terrain mapping. A number of variants have been proposed, including an Anglo/French model with extended range, but this was halted following the withdrawal of the UK. Others have included one fitted with a conventional warhead and even a long-range air-to-air missile specifically for attacking AEW aircraft, but none of these are believed to have been developed.

Refurbishment of the ASMP through an upgrade programme commenced in 1999 and will result in the missile with its 300 kT nuclear warhead remaining operational with the Mirage 2000N and Super Etendard for a number of years to come.

The ASMP is the French air-launched nuclear weapon.

TYPE: BA 102, 103 AND 104 LOW-DRAG GENERAL PURPOSE BOMBS

Manufacturer:	SEI
Country of manufacture:	Italy
Diameter:	10.75in (273mm)
Span:	15.4in (390mm)
Length:	7.12ft (2.17m)
Weight:	141lb (227kg)

An Italian 227kg BA 102 bomb.

The Italian BA family of low-drag GP bombs are built by SEI and are based on the US Mk.80. They have been built for use by high speed aircraft and are fitted with a streamlined nose to reduce drag.

There are three bombs in the BA family. The BA 102 weighs 227kg and is equivalent to the Mk.82. The 454kg BA 103 is equivalent to the Mk.83 and the 908kg BA 104 to the Mk.84. Their weights and dimensions are the same as their Mk.80 equivalent. A range of fuses and tails have been built appropriate to the mission requirements and they can be used with the Paveway system.

The BA family of bombs has been cleared for use with the AMX, MB-339 and the Tornado and is in current service with the Italian Air Force.

TYPE: BAP 100 AIRFIELD DENIAL AND CRATERING WEAPON

Manufacturer:	TDA (Thomson Brandt)
Country of manufacture:	France
Diameter:	3.94in (100mm)
Span:	4.33in (110mm)
Length:	5.84ft (1.78m)
Weight:	71.6lb (32.5kg)

The BAP 100 (*Bombe Accélérée de Pénétration*) is an airfield denial and cratering weapon developed by Thomson Brandt in the mid 1970s. It was designed to compete with the much larger Durandel.

The BAP 100 is carried on nine- or eighteen-round adapters and depending on the aircraft systems can be fired manually or totally automatically. Half a second after having been released, the missile deploys a parachute, which slows the weapon down and results in it pitching down. 3.75 seconds after release the weapon should have decelerated and now be at around 40 degrees to the ground. The booster is then fired and should hit the ground at around 260m/sec (418km/sec). The launcher is capable of firing all eighteen BAP 100s in around one second. By firing a quantity of these weapons in fast succession it is felt that there will be a higher chance of hitting the runway and creating more damage. The warhead is fitted with a piezo-electric sensor which ignites a pyrotechnic delay fuze. This results in the weapon exploding under the concrete, causing the runway to heave and be more difficult to repair. A quantity of the warheads can be fitted with delayed action to prevent repair teams moving in. Because of its size, the BAP 100 is a difficult weapon for EOD teams to locate, and due to its design it is virtually impossible to make safe.

BAP 100 has been cleared for use with A-4, Alpha Jet, F-5, Hawk, Jaguar, MB-326, MB-329, Mirage F.1, Mirage 2000, S.211 and the Super Etendard. It is in service in a number of air arms including the French Air Force, German Air Force, Greek Air Force and Portuguese Air Force.

A loaded pair of nine-round BAP 100 bomb carriers.

Manufacturer:	TDA (Thomson Brandt)
Country of manufacture:	France
Diameter:	4.72in (120mm)
Span:	4.72in (120mm)
Length:	4.92ft (1.5m)
Weight:	75lb (34kg)

The BAT 120 is an anti-armour weapon and is related to the similar looking BAP 100 anti-runway weapon.

The BAT 120 can be carried in the same nine- or eighteen-round launcher as the BAT 100. The initial launch is identical with the drag-chute opening half a second after launch. However, the similarity then ends. The weapon continues to slow down and 2.25 secs after launch it will be armed. By the time it reaches the ground it will be travelling at about 20m/sec. Upon touching the ground the fuze will trigger and the weapon will explode. There are two types of weapon available. One is the BAT 120AMV (anti-equipment and vehicle), which will explode into 2,600 calibrated fragments, each of which can pierce 4mm at 20m (0.16in at 65ft). The other is the BAT 120ABL (anti-light armoured vehicle), which will fragment into 800 calibrated fragments, each of which can pierce 7mm at 20m (0.27in at 65ft).

BAP 100 has been cleared for use with A-4, Alpha Jet, F-5, Hawk, Jaguar, MB-326, MB-329, Mirage F.1, Mirage 2000, S.211 and the Super Etendard. It is in service in a number of air arms including the French Air Force, German Air Force, Greek Air Force and Portuguese Air Force.

An unmarked Super Etendard armed with BAT 120 anti-armour bombs and R.550 Magic 2 air missiles under the wing.

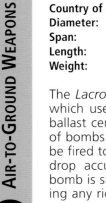

Manufacturer:	Lacroix
Country of manufacture:	France
Diameter:	3.88in (98.5mm)
Span:	4.33in (110mm)
Length:	2.96ft (902mm)
Weight:	35.27lb (16kg)

The *Lacroix Bavar* is a family of practice bombs which uses a modular system of nose, tail and ballast centre sections to simulate a wide range of bombs. On impact, a flare/smoke marker can be fired to assist spotting and assessment of the drop accuracy, while the construction of the bomb is such that it is destroyed, thereby avoiding any ricochets. The Bavar practice bombs are

Flat nose Bavar F3 and pointed F4 practice bombs in an LBF2 pod.

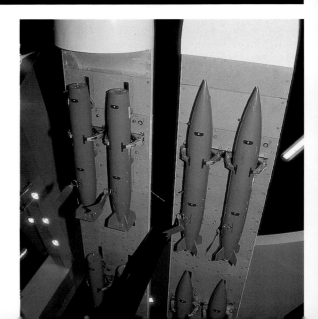

normally fitted into a pod which can be carried by Mirage, Jaguar, Alpha Jet, Epsilon and Super Etendard.

The F3 is a high-drag practice bomb that closely follows the trajectories of the SAMP and Matra 250 and 400kg bombs. The F4 is a low-drag practice bomb which closely resembles the French SAMP and *Matra Défence* 250kg and 500kg, as well as the US Mk.82 bombs. The shorter F7 is able to replicate the BAP 100, BAT 120, while the F9 can replicate the Durandal.

TYPE: BDU-33 PRACTICE BOMB

Manufacturer:	Various
Country of manufacture:	USA
Diameter:	4in (101mm)
Length:	24in (609mm)
Weight:	24.25lb (11kg)

The BDU-33 practice bomb is used by USAF and US Navy aircraft to represent the Mk.80 series of low-drag bombs and is used for training purposes. When it hits the ground a small smoke charge is ignited to aid locating. The BDU-33 may be in use with other operators of the Mk.80 bombs.

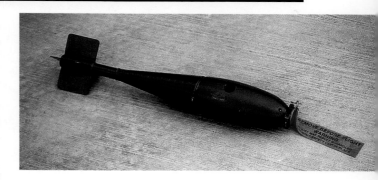

A BDU-33 practice bomb.

TYPE: BetAB-150/-250/-500 PENETRATION BOMBS

Manufacturer:	Not known
Country of manufacture:	Russia

The BetAB (*Betonoboynaya AviatsionnayaBbomba* or concrete-piercing aircraft bomb) is a Russian-built penetration bomb.

The BetAB has been built in three sizes with the number indicating the weight in the bomb. The BetAB-150 is 165kg, BetAB-250 250kg (illustrated) and the BetAB-500 447kg. There is also a BetAB-500ShP, which appeared to be designed for low-level operation as it is fitted with a rocket that would assist penetration.

It is probable that the BetAB bombs could be carried by most Russian strike aircraft such as the MiG-27, MiG-29 Su-24, Su-25 and Su-27. As operators of some of these aircraft they are likely to be on the inventory of the Czech, Hungarian and Polish Air Forces.

A BetAB-250 bomb which has been made safe by an EOD team.

TYPE: BGL BOMB

Manufacturer:	MBDA (Matra BAe Dynamics)
Country of manufacture:	France
Diameter:	15.9in (403mm)
Span:	4.7ft (1.43mm)
Length:	11.6ft (3.54m)
Weight:	1,036lb (470kg)

Matra developed their BGL (*Bombe a Guidage Laser* or Laser-Guided Bomb) during the late 1970s. It is similar in concept to the US Paveway system, requiring a laser designator, either from the ground or air, to illuminate the target. It also looks similar to the Paveway III, but has a distinct difference in that the seeker is separated from the The seeker locates the target and corrects the track of the bomb to ensure an accurate hit.

The 400kg BGL was the first of the family to be developed, followed by two other models, the

ABOVE: A BLG 400 ready for loading on to French Air Force Mirage 2000D at Istrana Air Base in Italy during operations against Serb targets. (Photo ECPA/J Marces via API)

250kg and 1,000kg. An additional special penetration variant named Arcole has also been built. Aerial designation would probably by the Altis pod which can either be fitted to the aircraft carrying the bomb or by another. The aircraft carrying the BGL can approach the target at high speed and at very low or medium altitudes (up to 15,000ft (4,570m)). The weapon is launched from a minimum stand-off range of 5 to 10km (3 to 6 miles), and is accurate up to a few metres.

Several air forces have ordered more than 1,750 GP and Penetration versions of the BGL. The weapon was used successfully in Bosnia (1994) and in the Balkans (1999) on the French Air Force Mirage 2000D.

As the BGL 400 is released from a Mirage 2000, the darker flip-out wings can be seen extended, which significantly increase the range of the LGB. (Photo CEV/Matra Défense via API)

TYPE: BGM-71 TOW MISSILE

Manufacturer:	Raytheon (Hughes)
Country of manufacture:	USA
Diameter:	6in (152mm)
Span:	18in (450m)
Length:	46in (1.17m)
Weight:	50lb (22.7kg)
Range:	2.5 miles (4km)

Development of the BGM-71 TOW (Tube-launched Optically tracked, Wire-guided) missile was commenced by Hughes in the mid 1960s. It became operational in 1970 and was first used in Vietnam.

Once a target has been spotted and locked on using a roof-mounted or MMS (Mast-Mounted Sight) the missile can be launched. The guidance control constantly measures the distance of the missile from the line of sight and transmits the appropriate corrective commands down a trailed cable to the missile.

Highly successful, the initial TOW model was the BGM-71A, which was followed by an improved range BGM-71B. The BGM-71C

Improved TOW featured a 381mm (15in) probe and an increased ability to penetrate armour. The BGM-71D continued this theme and featured a longer probe and larger warhead amongst a number of improvements. A significant improvement to the missile resulted in the BGM-71E TOW 2A which would attack the weaker top of armoured vehicles such as MBTs and defeat reactive armour. The BGM-71F TOW 2B and features a flat nose.

The latest model is the TOW F&F. It is fitted with an advanced focal plane array imaging infrared seeker. This missile sees the target and information from the seeker is used to guide the weapon on to the target. Due to this capability, the need for a trailing wire is eliminated, although a wireless man-in-the-loop capability remains available. The wireless feature also results in an increased range.

The TOW missile is the standard anti-tank missile for the AH-1 of the US Army and USMC. It is used to arm the British Army Lynx and can be fitted to a

A quad BGM-71 TOW launcher plus an M260 rocket launcher pod with Hydra 70 rockets.

number of other helicopters including the Bo105, Agusta A109 and A129 and the Hughes 500 family. TOW is widely used throughout the world including Belgium, Denmark, Italy and UK.

TYPE: BL 61 FRAGMENTATION BOMB

Manufacturer:	SAMP
Country of manufacture:	France
Diameter:	8.6in (219mm)
Span:	10.6in (270mm)
Length:	4.36ft (1.33m)
Weight:	276lb (125kg)

The BL 61 is a fragmentation bomb built by SAMP. It uses a forging technique that creates a pattern and thus produces the required degree of fragmentation.

As with others of the BL family of bombs, the BL 61 has standard NATO lugs and can be carried by most combat aircraft. It is used by the French Air Force.

SAMP 125kg BL 61 bombs on a triple carrier.

TYPE: BL 70 FRAGMENTATION BOMB

Manufacturer:	SAMP
Country of manufacture:	France
Diameter:	12.75in (324mm)
Span:	7.72in (450mm)
Length:	7.32ft (2.23m)
Weight:	882lb (400kg)

The 400kg BL-70 with a MF BF nose kit, plus others in the range of the French SAMP bombs. Data is for the BL-70-MF BF.

The French BL bombs produced by SAMP cover a range of types, with most available in a series of sizes to meet a diverse number of roles.

The BL 70 is a 400kg fragmentation bomb with an internal case finish to optimize its maximum fragmentation on detonation. A 120kg BL 25A and 125kg BL 61 make this a range of bomb for use against soft targets.

BL EU2 250KG BOMB

Manufacturer:	SAMP
Country of manufacture:	France
Diameter:	10.7in (273mm)
Span:	15in (380mm)
Length:	7.6ft (2.31m)
Weight:	507lb (230kg)

The BL EU are a group of three 250kg bombs which appear similar but fulfil different roles. Of a similar appearance, the EU2 is for general purpose, the EU2FR is a fragmentation model and the EU2P is a penetration weapon with a pointed nose. It is fitted with a post-impact fuse and is capable of penetrating 1.1m or reinforced concrete prior to exploding.

The 250kg BL EU2 low drag general purpose bomb is the French equivalent of the Mk.82 and can be fitted with the Paveway II LGB kit to create a PGM.

ABOVE: The BL EU2 bomb fitted with the MFBF nose and a tail arming vane. Behind is another EU2 with a US BSU-49B Ballute retarding tail and the nose fuse exposed. Behind that is the EU2P which is the penetration bomb variant. Data is for the EU2-MF-BF.

BELOW: The 250kg EU2 with Paveway II.

BL755 CLUSTER BOMB

Manufacturer:	Hunting Engineering
Country of manufacture:	UK
Diameter:	17.6in (447mm)
Span:	2.33ft (710mm)
Length:	8.04ft (2.45m)
Weight:	610lb (277kg)

The Hunting BL755 cluster bomb was developed in the late 1960s to meet an RAF requirement for a Cluster Bomb Unit (CBU) for use against soft and hard targets.

BL755 contains 147 shaped charge bomblets and uses a gas-generating cartridge to release the outer casing and eject the bomblets. Two types of bomblet can be fitted into these CBUs. The BL755 No. 1 is armed with a general purpose munition which has a petal-like tail and is designed primarily for use against soft targets such as aircraft, SAMs and unarmoured vehicles using a fragmen-

tation warhead. It has a limited capability against armour. The CBU No. 2 (or IBL-755) is specifically for use against armoured vehicles. These

A BL755 CBU on an RAF Harrier GR.7.

An RBL755 CBU on an RAF Harrier GR.7 during operations against Serb targets. It is recognizable by the small protuberances on the tail section.

Submunitions from the BL755 No.1 (illustrated) and the No.2 bomblets.

bomblets are fitted with a parachute to give a higher impact angle and have a high velocity jet that is triggered on impact and can burn a hole through armour. These BL755s are designed for release at low level and the bomblets would be distributed over an area 150m long and 60m wide (490ft x 200ft).

Development of the BL755 system has led to the RBL755 and BL755PS. RBL755 is similar to the standard BL755, but is designed for medium-level launch and is fitted with a ground-detecting sensor to ensure separation of the bomblets at the optimum height over the target. The BL755PS is fitted with a Doppler radar

and can be used at high or medium level or tossed from low level. The Doppler ensures separation at the optimum height over the target. A kit has been produced to enable the Mk.3 ground-sensing capability to be retrofitted to the earlier models.

The BL755 is a free-fall weapon and so can be carried by virtually any aircraft with the standard NATO fitting lugs. It is used by the RAF on the Harrier GR.7/T.4 and T.10, Hawk T.1, Jaguar GR.1 and T.2/4, Tornado GR.1/4 and can be carried on the Royal Navy Sea Harrier FA.2. BL755 is also in service with eight other NATO countries as well as others around the world.

TYPE: BLG 66 BELOUGA CLUSTER BOMB

Manufacturer:	SAMP
Country of manufacture:	France
Diameter:	14.4in (366mm)
Length:	10.83ft (3.3m)
Weight:	672lb (305kg)

The Belouga CBU was developed by Thomson Brandt and Matra in the mid 1970s. It is similar in appearance to a low-drag bomb, but with a pattern indicating the apertures for the submunitions. One hundred and fifty-one submunitions can be fitted and these are available in three types – general purpose fragmentation for use against soft targets, anti-armour for tanks and APCs, and an interdiction model effective againt concrete structures such as roads and runways. The pilot has two options for the ground pattern, which can be set in flight prior to release. This can be either be a long pattern (240m (787ft)) or short and dense

(120m (394ft)). In both cases the pattern is 40m (130ft) wide.

The Belouga CBU entered service with the French Air Force at the end of the 1970s for use on their Mirage and Jaguars and have been exported to several other countries including Greece and Turkey.

The Belouga cluster bomb, identifiable by the unusual spotted appearance indicating the exit ports for the 151 submunitions. Amongst the other weapons on display with the AMX is the eighteen-round BAP 100 bomb carrier.

BLU-109/B BOMB

Manufacturer:	Lockheed Martin
Country of manufacture:	USA
Diameter:	14.57in (370mm)
Length:	7ft 10.5in (2.4m)
Weight:	1,927lb (874kg)

The 2,000lb BLU-109 has been developed by Lockheed Martin to defeat the enemy's most critical and hardened targets, including secure command bunker locations, weapon storage as well as key transport and communications. The BLU-109's advanced technology hardened steel case penetrates the target intact, enabling it to get to the interior of hardened targets, where the warhead explodes, thus ensuring target destruction.

BLU-109 can be delivered as either an unguided or, more likely, a guided weapon and has therefore been cleared for use with a variety of combat-proven precision guidance systems including Paveway, GBU-15 and AGM-130.

The BLU-109 bomb showing the nose adaptor ring for fitting a Paveway kit.

BLU-109 is currently in production and is operational with the USAF on a variety of aircraft including the A-10, B-1, B-2 and F-15. It is also being built under licence and used by other air forces.

BME 330 CLUSTER BOMB

Manufacturer:	Expal
Country of manufacture:	Spain
Diameter:	13.8in (350mm)
Span:	1.9ft (580mm)
Length:	7.38ft (2.25m)
Weight:	699lb (317kg)

Expal began development of the BME 330 family of CBUs in the early 1990s.

The BME 330 CBU family comprises three weapons optimized for specific missions. The BME 330 AR (Anti-Runway) contains twenty-eight SAP bomblets. These are scattered from the container and on impact fire their first explosion, which creates a small crater. This enables the second charge to take advantage of the weakness and can result in the penetration of up to 600mm (23in) of concrete. The second charge may be on a timer and so can prevent access to repair the runway.

The second model is the BME 330 AT (Anti-Tank), which contains 516 SAC-1 submunitions. An option is to replace four of the SAC-1s with a similar number of MAC-2 AT mines. Again, this is a two-charge submunition and it is claimed to be able to penetrate up to 100mm (4in) of steel plate. The third model is the BME 330 C (multi-purpose) and this contains a total of 180 anti-personnel, anti-armour and area denial submunitions. While the anti-personnel and anti-armour submunitions will detonate immediately on landing in the area, denial munitions will be programmed to take up to 24 hours to detonate.

The BME 330 CBU are in service with the Spanish Air Force and Navy and have been cleared for use on the EAV-8B, EF-18, F-5 and Mirage F.1.

A sectioned BME 330 cluster bomb with the submunitions visible.

BR50, BR125, BR250 AND BR500 BOMBS

Manufacturer:	Expal
Country of manufacture:	Spain
Diameter:	11.3in (290mm)
Span:	17.2in (440mm)
Length:	7.1ft (2.15m)
Weight:	551lb (250kg)

The Expal BR family of low-drag bombs follows the same pattern as the Mk.80 family.

The basic BL family is of the fragmentation type although there is also a smoke model. A number of variants have been built including the BRFA 330 penetration bomb, which has a hardened steel nose, a rocket motor and is fitted with a brake-chute. Also built is the BRP, which is fitted with a brake-chute and is available in various sizes. A subsequent improved variant capable of being dropped at speed and altitudes down to 18m (60ft) is designated BRP.S. In each case, the number after the letters indicates the weight of the bomb.

Spanish BR-250 bombs displayed with an RAF Harrier GR.7 to represent their use by the Spanish Navy with their AV-8B Harriers.

The BL bombs have been cleared for use on AV-8B, F-5, EF-18 and Mirage F1 and are in use with the Spanish Air Force and Navy.

BRIMSTONE MISSILE

Manufacturer:	MBDA (Alenia Marconi Systems)
Country of manufacture:	UK
Diameter:	7in (178mm)
Length:	5.94ft (1.81m)
Weight:	107lb (48.5kg)
Max speed:	Supersonic
Range:	5 miles+ (8km+)

The Brimstone anti-armour missile is a British development of the Hellfire missile that was commenced by GEC Marconi in the mid 1980s. It uses the same body as the AGM-114K, but has been fitted with a new active radar seeker and strengthened to enable it to be carried by fast jets.

Brimstone anti-armour missiles on triple launchers under the wing of an RAF Harrier GR.7.

This new seeker and its digital processor can detect, acquire and identify APCs, SAMs, tanks, small ships, parked helicopters and aircraft, and the missile can be programmed to select a particular target from several options. Even when fired as a salvo they can be programmed to hit separate targets Brimstone has a tandem HEAT warhead, the same warhead used in the AGM-114L version. However, due to its modular construction this could be changed to another such as fragmentation if required. A special three-missile launcher assembly has been developed for fitting Brimstone missiles to fixed-wing high-speed aircraft, and this launcher weighs 85kg (187lb).

Following Operation Allied Force against the former Yugoslavia, there was a changing requirement for use of Brimstone in a low-intensity operation. This has led to an interest in a laser-guided variant which would provide a lock-on prior to launch as opposed to the current configuration which can be fired with lock-on or in a search-and-detect mode.

In 1996 Brimstone was selected by the RAF for use with their Tornado and Harrier with a capability of fitting twelve missiles. Once in service, a total of eighteen missiles can be carried by the Eurofighter and it may also be carried by the British Army Apache. It is also suitable for integration with the F-16, F/A-18, Gripen, F-5 and L-159 aircraft as well as combat helicopters.

CBU-52B CLUSTER BOMB

Manufacturer:	Various
Country of manufacture:	USA
Diameter:	17in (430mm)
Span:	1ft 11in (580mm)
Length:	7ft 7.75in (2.33m)
Weight:	816lb (370kg)

The CBU-52 is one example of the loaded SUU-30. It is filled with 254 of the BLU-61/B fragmentation/incendiary bomblets and each of these bomblets weighs approximately 1kg (2.2lb) and is spherical in shape. A substantial number of the CBU-52B/B were dropped by US aircraft during the Gulf War.

The SUU-30 is in service with the USAF and can be dropped by most NATO attack aircraft. As a result it may well be in service with some other air arms.

A CBU-52/B cluster bomb under the wing of a USAF A-10 Thunderbolt II.

CBU-87 COMBINED EFFECTS MUNITION (CEM)/CLUSTER BOMB

Manufacturer:	Alliant/Olin
Country of manufacture:	USA
Diameter:	15.6in (396mm)
Span:	3ft 6in (1.07m)
Length:	7ft 8in (2.34m)
Weight:	950lb (431kg)

The Alliant CBU-87 Combined Effects Munition (CEM) is an all-purpose Cluster Bomb Unit (CBU) which entered production in 1984.

The CBU-87 is based on the Tactical Munitions Dispenser (TMD). This is a free-fall dispenser that can be dropped from virtually any USAF tactical or strategic aircraft at altitudes from 200 to 40,000ft (60–12,190m) and at speeds from 200–700kts and filled with a number of submunition types. It has a proximity sensor and can be adjusted to tailor the ground pattern size and shape to the target. The CBU-87/B contains 202 of the Combined Effects Bomblets (CEB) designated BLU-97, with a triple charge featuring a shaped charge capable of defeating armour, a fragmenting case for soft vehicles as well as an incendiary device. The spread of the submunitions can destroy targets in an area of 200 x 400m (656 x 1,312ft).

The CBU-87/B can be carried by the A-10, F-15, F-16 and B-52 of the USAF, and 10,035 were expended during the Gulf War.

The existence of the CBU-94 cluster bomb came to light during the Kosovo operations when it was used against Serb electrical power generation and distribution systems. The container is probably similar to that used by the CBU-87 or CBU-97, which is described elsewhere. The submunition is the BLU-114, which appears to contain a quantity of a carbon-graphite threads. These are probably dispersed by a small explosive charge while airborne and the threads then produce a shorting conductor over an inside the installation, causing shorting and overheating and leading to major interruption to power supplies.

CBU-87 CEM cluster bomb on a 494th FS, 48th FW, F-15E Strike Eagle. Also visible is an AIM-120 AMRAAM air-to-air missile and just visible is the drooping gimballed seeker of a Paveway II.

Manufacturer:	Textron
Country of manufacture:	USA
Diameter:	16in (406mm)
Length:	7ft 8in (2.34m)
Weight:	927lb (421kg)

A sectioned CBU-97/B SFW on display showing the BLU-108 submunitions.

The Textron Sensor-Fuzed Weapon (SFW) is a cluster bomb designated CBU-97 by the US Armed Forces. It is the first smart munition to enter service with the USAF and comprises an SUU-64 munition dispenser containing ten BLU-108 submunitions. Each of these submunitions is armed with four smart Skeet warheads, each of which is fitted with a dual-mode passive infrared and active laser sensor. Each of the Skeet warheads is capable of defeating a land combat vehicle.

The CBU-97 can be modified by removing the tail unit and fitting the Lockheed Martin Wind-Corrected Munition Dispenser (WCMD) kit, and is then redesignated CBU-105. This variant can be used at altitudes of up to 40,000ft (12,190m),

The BLU-108 submunition showing the four smart heat-seeking warheads. (Photo Textron Systems via API)

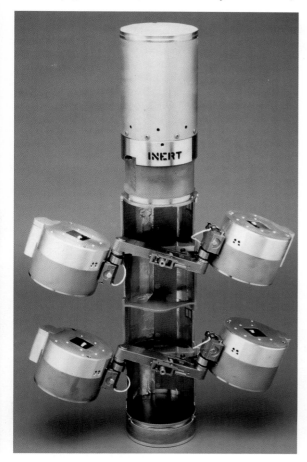

when it has a stand-off range of up to 10 miles (16km). While the aircraft launching the CBU-97 can be any with the appropriate 14in bomb rack, the CBU-105 requires some information prior to being dropped. Once launched, the ten BLU-108s are released at a predetermined altitude irrespective of weather conditions. Each of the BLU-108s is fitted with four Skeet warheads and as the unit spins on a small parachute these use their sensors to locate, track and attack targets which meet defined characteristics. Once a target has been located, the Skeet fires an Explosively Formed Penetrator (EFP). This is capable of penetrating tanks and APCs. At the same time as the EFP core is fired, a projectile fragmentation ring is also fired, which is lethal for soft targets that may be close by. In total, the CBU-97 or CBU-105 is capable of covering approximately 30 acres (1,307,000sq ft/121,000sq m).

The CBU-97/CBU-105 has also been designed with consideration for post-battle EOD clearance in mind. Each of the Skeet warheads has a self-destruct instruction should a target not be detected. Should this not function, the warhead would automatically deactivate after a set period.

The CBU-97 has been cleared for use with most USAF tactical aircraft including the A-10, B-1, B-2, B-52, F-15E and F-16, and can be used from most aircraft with bomb racks capable of carrying 1,000lb bombs. It can be dropped at any height from 200 to 20,000ft (60–6,100ft) and at any speed up to 650kts. The SFW is in full production, with deliveries having commenced in 1994 and over half of the current USAF inventory objective of 5,000 weapons having been ordered.

AIR-TO-GROUND WEAPONS

Manufacturer:	MBDA (Matra)
Country of manufacture:	International France/UK
Diameter:	8.78in (223mm)
Span:	16.93in (430mm)
Length:	8.86ft (2.7m)
Weight:	430lb (195kg)

The Durandal was developed as a runway penetration bomb by Matra in the early 1970s to meet a French Air Force requirement.

The Durandal is released from the carrier aircraft and a small brake-chute is deployed. Once clear of the aircraft, a timer releases the main parachute to reduce its speed dramatically. When the bomb reaches an angle of 30 degrees, the parachute is released and the solid rocket motor ignites to accelerate the bomb quickly to around 250m/s (400km/s). It then literally smashes its way through up to 400mm (16in) of concrete and a timer delay detonates the warhead from under the concrete, causing heave that will lift great chunks of the runway. It is also possible to adjust the time so that the explosion can take place some hours later, thus holding up any repairs to the airfield.

The Durandal is in service with the USAF as the BLU-107/B.

The Durandal is fitted with standard NATO attachment lugs and can therefore be carried by most attack aircraft. Besides being used by the French Air Force, it was ordered for in the USAF as the BLU-107/B and has served with numerous other countries.

Manufacturer:	Bazalt
Country of manufacture:	Russia
Diameter:	12.6in (320m)
Span:	12.6in (320m)
Length:	4.86ft (1.48m)
Weight:	516lb (234kg)

The FAB (*Fugasnaya Avia Bomba* or aerial demolition bomb) comprises a family of high-explosive bombs with an ancestry going back well before World War II.

According to the designation, FAB-250M-54 is a 250kg bomb which entered service in 1954. Other bombs in this range are the 500kg FAB-500M-54 and the large 1,500kg FAB-1500M-54. These bombs have standard lugs and can be carried by most attack aircraft including the MiG-21, MiG-27, MiG-29, Su-24, Su-25, Su-27 and Su-30. The FAB-1500M-54 is most likely to be carried only by the larger bombers such as the Tu-22, Tu-95 and Tu-160.

All three bombs are in service with Russian forces, but other operators of any of these types will probably only use the two smaller weapons. NATO operators are the Czech, Hungarian and Polish Air Forces.

Six FAB-250M-54 bombs on the centreline pylon of a Su-30.

GATOR MINE SYSTEM

Manufacturer:	Olin
Country of manufacture:	USA
Diameter:	16in (406mm)
Span:	3ft 6in (1.07m)
Length:	7ft 8in (2.34m)
Weight:	710lb (322kg)

The Gator mine system was developed by Aerojet in the mid 1980s with new BLU-91 anti-tank and BLU-92 anti-personnel mines and to utilize existing Suspended Underwing Units (SUU) submunition containers.

The Gator system has been fitted to a number of containers with different permutations of mines fitted. The US Navy and Air Force also have their own model of a similar weapon and each has been given its own designation. These include the CBU-78, CBU-83, CBU-84, CBU-85, CBU-86 and CBU-89. The USAF CBU-89 and US Navy CBU-78 have been built in the most significant numbers and are based on the SUU-64 and Mk.7 Rockeye containers respectively. These are unguided munitions that have a wide spread and can be dropped reasonably accurately at lower levels, while becoming progressively less accurate at higher altitudes. As a result, Lockheed Martin have developed the Wind-Corrected Munitions Dispenser (see separate entry).

The Gator system has been cleared for use with most US attack aircraft and is in service with the USAF, US Navy and USMC.

A Gator mine dispenser uses the SUU-64 container, making it a CBU-89.

AS-10 'KAREN' (KH-25) MISSILE

Manufacturer:	Zvezda-Strela
Country of manufacture:	Russia
Diameter:	10.83in (275mm)
Span:	2.56ft (780mm)
Length:	14.11ft (4.3m)
Weight:	705lb (320kg)
Range:	24.9 miles (40km)

The Kh-25M is a short-range air-to-ground missile that commenced development in the 1960s. It has been built with laser homing (Kh-25ML), TV (Kh-25MT), IR (Kh-25 MTP) and active radar (Kh-25MA) guidance systems. These missiles can be fired as single shots or as a salvo. In addition to being capable of being carried by most current Russian attack aircraft, they can also be fitted on advanced training aircraft as well as single-seat attack helicopters.

The latest variant of the Kh-25M is the Kh-MPU (illustrated), which is designed for the SEAD role as a short-to-medium range anti-radar missile that can be carried by the Su-25, Su-27 and Ka-52. It is a further development of the Kh-25MP, using the motor, communications and warhead modules but fitted with a passive wideband homing seeker designed to locate air defence radar transmissions. Once located, the information is

A Kh-25MPU on display at the Paris Air Show.

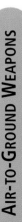

AIR-TO-GROUND WEAPONS

61

This laser guided variant of the AS-10 Karen is designated Kh-25ML by the Russian manufacturers.

passed to the missile autopilot which keeps the missile on track even if the radar is switched off. This variant was allocated the NATO reporting designation of AS-12 'Kegler'.

With the exception of the Kh-25MPU, all other variants of the Kh-25 were allocated the NATO reporting designation of AS-10 'Karen'. The Kh-25 can be carried by most current Russian attack aircraft and is currently in service with many former Warsaw Pact air forces including those of the Czech Republic, Bulgaria and Poland.

TYPE:	BLU-82 DAISY CUTTER / COMMANDO VAULT

Country of manufacture	USA
Diameter	4ft 6in (1.37m)
Length	15ft 10.6in (4.84m)
Weight loaded	15000lb (6810 kg)

The BLU-82 originally saw service in Vietnam where it was referred to as Commando Vault. It was used as a blast bomb where its effect proved useful for clearing instant helicopter landing sites in the jungle. It was designed as a replacement for the 10,000lb (4540kgs) M121 bombs that were left over from WW2. A total of 225 were built by the USAF.

The BLU-82 comprises of 15,000lb (6810kgs) bomb containing 12,600lb (5720kgs) of explosive which is dropped from a Hercules aircraft. Because of its weight and shape, this bomb cannot be fitted in the bomb bay of any bomber aircraft. The bomb comprises of a cylindrical section with a conical nose with a 4ft 1in (1.24m) long probe containing the fuse. It is launched from the Hercules using a cargo extractor pallet. Once clear of the Hercules the pallet separates and a parachute is deployed. The bomb floats down and when the probe strikes the ground the fuse is detonated. The effect of the explosive blast of the BLU-82 is designed to be effective horizontally and with minimal vertical blast. This results in a jungle clearing several hundred feet wide and no crater.

During the Gulf War a total of eleven BLU-82s were dropped, mainly on Iraqi minefields. Further examples which were referred to as Daisy Cutters were dropped on Taliban/Al Qa'ida positions during the operation to destroy the terrorist cave complexes in Afghanistan during 2001.

The BLU-82 is currently only cleared to be dropped from the MC-130H Combat Talon variant of the Hercules. This aircraft is operated by USAF Special Operations Command.

The BLU-82 strapped onto a cargo extractor pallet. The simple cylindrical section and conical nose can be clearly seen but the probe contailing the fuse has not been fitted. (Photo USAF SOC)

The rear view of the BLU-82 shows the parachute pack and attachments which are used to slow the bomb and to maintain its correct attitude with the nose pointing vertically down. (Photo USAF SOC)

Manufacturer: Raytheon (Texas)
Country of manufacture: USA

The Paveway I system of Laser-Guided Bombs (LGB) was originally developed by Texas Instruments in the mid 1960s in conjunction with the Armament Development and Test Center at Eglin AFB.

The Paveway comprises a kit with a nose and tail section that can be fitted to standard bombs and requires no special connections to the aircraft. The nose-mounted seeker searches for a coded laser reflection from the target and once detected steers the bomb on to the illuminated target. The source for the laser designation can be the launch aircraft or another aircraft, or can come from a designator on the ground. The first of these LGBs was dropped in April 1965 and by the early 1970s the family had grown to include seekers for a number of bombs.

Initial Paveway production commenced in 1968 with a seeker for the 750lb M117 bomb, which was then tested in Vietnam. As expected, accuracy was far greater than for the standard iron bomb.

Development of Paveway I commenced in the mid 1970s. It comprised a number of kits including the KMU-342 for the 750lb Mk.117 bomb, KMU-370 for the 3,000lb Mk.118, KMU-388 for the 500lb Mk.82, KMU-421 for the 1,000lb Mk.83 and KMU-351 for the 2,000lb Mk.84. The latter was designated GBU-10A and KBU-388 became the GBU-12A.

Production continued until 1979, by which time substantial quantities had been delivered to the USAF and US Navy. A number of other countries ordered these LGBs including Greece and Turkey.

Some of the family of Paveway II LGBs.
(Photo Raytheon via API)

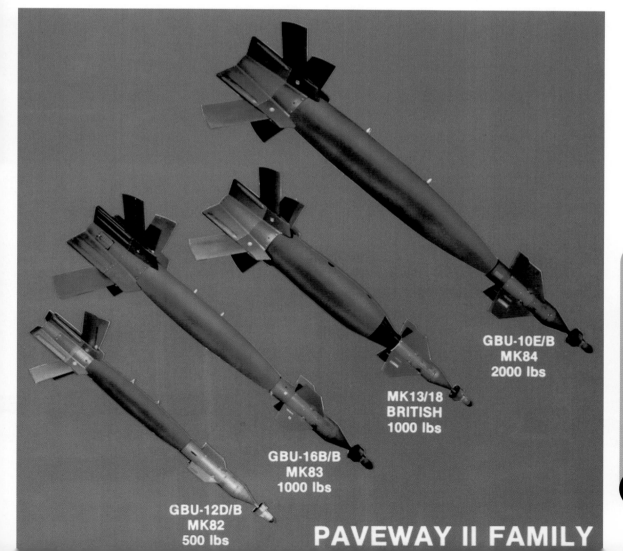

GBU-10E/B
MK84
2000 lbs

MK13/18
BRITISH
1000 lbs

GBU-16B/B
MK83
1000 lbs

GBU-12D/B
MK82
500 lbs

PAVEWAY II FAMILY

The Paveway II was developed to rectify some of the shortcomings of the earlier system. This included a small wing that flipped out after launch to increase the glide range and an increase in the sensitivity of the seeker.

The Paveway II comprises the GBU-10E with the Mk.84 bomb, the GBU-12D with the Mk.82 and the GBU-16B with the Mk.83.

Paveway III began development in the early 1980s to rectify the main source of concern, which was the short glide distance when dropped at low level. Larger wings were fitted and improvement to the guidance gave greater flexibility for the carrier aircraft.

The Paveway III comprises the GBU-22 with the Mk.82 bomb, GBU-24 with the Mk.84 or BLU-109 bombs, GBU-27 with the BLU-113 and GBU-28 with its special warhead.

These improvements for Paveway III came at a substantial cost and the US Navy therefore decided to produce the Skipper – a Paveway II with a rocket motor. The UK has also built its own Paveway system, designated Paveway II (UK) and Paveway III (UK). Both of these are covered separately.

All three basic models of Paveway have been acquired in substantial numbers for the US armed forces. Exports have also been substantial to a large number of countries throughout the world, and Paveway remains in service in most if not all of the NATO countries.

GBU-10 Paveway II LGB Bomb

Manufacturer:	Raytheon (Texas)
Country of manufacture:	USA
Diameter:	18in (460mm)
Span:	5ft 6in (1.68m)
Length:	14ft 4in (4.37m)
Weight:	2,562lb (1,163kg)

A pair of 2,000lb GBU-10s under the wing of an F-111F with an AIM-9 Sidewinder. When the 48th FW at RAF Lakenheath replaced the F-111 with the F-15E, they continued to fly the GBU-10s.

A GBU-10 with the 2,000lb Mk.84 bomb.

GBU-12 Paveway II LGB Bomb

Manufacturer:	Raytheon (Texas)
Country of manufacture:	USA
Diameter:	10.75in (273mm)
Span:	4ft 4.75in (1.34m)
Length:	10ft 11in (3.33m)
Weight:	500lb (227kg)

The GBU-12 with the 500lb Mk.82 bomb.

GBU-22/B Paveway III LGB bomb

Manufacturer:	Raytheon (Texas)
Country of manufacture:	USA
Diameter:	10.8in (275mm)
Span:	4ft 7in (1.4m)
Length:	11ft 6in (3.5m)
Weight:	718lb (326kg)

The GBU-22 is the Paveway III model armed with a 500lb Mk.82 bomb.

GBU-24/B Paveway III LGB Bomb

Manufacturer:	Raytheon (Texas)
Country of manufacture:	USA
Diameter:	18in (460mm)
Span:	6ft 6.75in (2m)
Length:	14ft 5in (4.39m)
Weight:	2,000lb (908kg)

GBU-24A/B Paveway III LGB Bomb

Manufacturer:	Raytheon (Texas)
Country of manufacture:	USA
Diameter:	14.5in (370mm)
Span:	6ft 8in (2.03m)
Length:	14ft 2in (4.31m)
Weight:	2,348lb (1,066kg)

The GBU-24/B Paveway III LGB uses the 2,000lb Mk.84 bomb as the warhead. It originally entered service with the USAF in 1985, followed by the US Navy in 1992. A total of 1,181 GBU-24s were dropped during the Gulf War.

GBU-24A/B has a high-penetration capability which is achieved with the BLU-109 ammunition.

GBU-27/B Paveway III LGB Penetration Bomb

Manufacturer:	Lockheed Martin
Country of manufacture:	USA
Diameter:	14.57in (370mm)
Span:	5ft 6in (1.68m)
Length:	13ft 11in (4.24m)
Weight:	2,170lb (985kg)

The GBU-27/B is a highly accurate LGB used by the F-117 Nighthawk which entered service with the USAF in 1988. It is basically a GBU-24A/B Paveway III LGB with the BLU-109 bomb, but modified to fit in the F-117 bomb bay. The modifications include using the GBU-10 tail and having shorter adapter rings. It is also coated with Radar-Absorbing Material (RAM) to reduce the radar signature prior to dropping the bomb and while the F-117's bomb doors are open.

A variant of the GBU-27 is the EGBU-27, which incorporates GPS to provide an improved poor-weather capability to locate the target accurately.

A GBU-27/B Paveway III penetration bomb without its seeker being loaded into a USAF F-117A Nighthawk stealth fighter.
(Photo Lockheed Martin via API)

GBU-28/B Paveway III LGB Penetration Bomb

Manufacturer:	Lockheed Martin
Country of manufacture:	USA
Diameter:	14in (356mm)
Span:	5ft 6in (1.68m)
Length:	19ft 2in (5.84m)
Weight:	4,676lb (2,123kg)

The GBU-28/B Paveway III LGB is designed specifically for attacks on hardened targets. It was quickly developed in just seventeen days prior to the Gulf War under the USAF's rapid response programme. The bomb is modified from an obsolete 8in gun barrel which is sealed and filled with explosive. A GBU-24 nose and tail LGB guidance system is fitted and completed with a BLU-113 penetration warhead.

It is reported that just thirty of these bombs were built. Two were used during trials and a further two used against Iraqi targets. These were delivered by F-111Fs of the 48th TFW at supersonic speed to increase their kinetic speed. They had the ability to penetrate 100ft (30m) of earth or 20ft (6m) of concrete.

It is also reported that a further batch of GBU-28s have been ordered. Proposals were made for an EGBU-28 which was fitted with GPS and an additional pair of wings. It is uncertain if any of these were part of this or any subsequent order. The GBU-28/B can be carried by the F-15E, B-1B and B-2.

The GBU-28/B Paveway III LGB penetration bomb is capable of penetrating 100ft of earth or 20 ft of concrete.

TYPE:	PAVEWAY II (UK) LGB BOMB

Manufacturer:	Portsmouth Aviation
Country of manufacture:	UK
Diameter:	29.26in (743.2mm)
Span:	5.47ft (1.667m)
Length:	11.44ft (3.488m)
Weight:	1,228lb (557kg)

During the 1970s the RAF issued a requirement for a laser-guided bomb. As a result, a programme was implemented to modify the existing and successful Texas Instruments kit to fit the RAF 1,000lb HE bombs. These kits are adapted for use by Portsmouth Aviation. These kits comprise the US-built Computer Control Group nose section and a No. 120 Tail Unit which has retractable fins. Portsmouth Aviation manufacture an adapter for the nose section and another for the tail section. These enable the US kits to be fitted with a smooth airflow over the whole weapon. The tail section also houses the Multi-Function Bomb Fuse (MFBF).

The Paveway requires laser designation to enable the seeker heat to guide the bomb on to the target. This can be provided by a TIALD pod carried by the launching aircraft or another aircraft, or from a ground-based designator. The laser light has a code enabling several LGBs to be dropped on a number of targets in close proximity simultaneously. Should the LGB fail to locate the laser designation, the bomb will fall as a standard iron dumb bomb.

The Paveway II (UK) entered service with the RAF towards the end on the 1970s and was used in small numbers in the Falklands, and has been used since during the Gulf War and in the former Yugoslavia.

The Paveway II (UK) is carried by the RAF Harrier, Jaguar and Tornado.

The Paveway II (UK) with a 1,000lb ATS insert training bomb attached to the centreline pylon of an RAF Jaguar.

TYPE:	PAVEWAY III (UK) LGB BOMB

Manufacturer:	Portsmouth Aviation
Country of manufacture:	UK
Diameter:	14.57in (370mm)
Span:	6.72ft (2.048m)
Length:	14.58ft (4.445m)
Weight:	Up to 2,549lb (1,156kg)

Following the success of the Paveway II (UK) LGB, an improved and more powerful Paveway III (UK) was developed, based on the Raytheon Paveway III and using BLU-109 as the munition.

Portsmouth Aviation modify the tail unit to accommodate a new Multi-Function Bomb Fuze and adapter rings for the nose and tail. Unlike the UK Paveway II, this model uses proportional guidance – the control canards move only the exact amount necessary to guide the weapon. An autopilot flies the weapon from its release to the target using one of several flight profiles. These profiles are designed to provide the best attack conditions for different types of target and also allow the UK Paveway III to be released at greater ranges from the target than the Paveway II. The Paveway III (UK) is capable of penetrating over 1.5m (5ft) of reinforced concrete, which makes it very effective against hardened targets.

The Paveway III (UK) entered service in 1998 was used during Operation Desert Fox and in operations against Serb targets in Kosovo and Serbia.

The Paveway III (UK) is carried by RAF Harrier, Jaguar and Tornado and will be carried by the Typhoon.

A Paveway III (UK) fitted to an RAF Harrier GR.7 during operations against Serb targets.

Manufacturer:	Raytheon (Texas)
Country of manufacture:	USA
Diameter:	18in (460mm)
Span:	4ft 11in (1.5m)
Length:	12ft 11in (3.94m)
Weight:	2,513lb (1,140kg)
Range:	5 miles (8km)

The GBU-15 or Cruciform Wing Weapon (CWW) is a modular electro-optically guided glide bomb developed in the mid 1970s. It entered production with Rockwell in the early 1980s.

The GBU-15 comprises a target-sensing device mounted on the front of a 2,000lb bomb with trajectory control fins attached to the rear. The 2,000lb Mk.84 bomb is the normal warhead used, but it can also be the BLU-109 penetration bomb. With TV guidance it is designated AGM-15(V)1/B. If fitted with the IR nose, this becomes the CBU-15(V)2/B. A third but less common variant is the GBU-15(V)3/B which uses the CBU-75. Target detection can be either a TV or IR device with the image transmitted via a data link. The GBU-15 can be launched at medium to low altitudes. With low-level releases, the bomb will climb until the target is acquired. It is then either guided by the weapons systems operator in the aircraft on to the target or it locks on the homing head. For higher-level launches the bomb flies a line-of-sight attack. In both scenarios the launch aircraft can be making its escape.

The GBU-15 was fitted to the F-4 and F-111, the latter dropping seventy GBU-15s during the Gulf War. They are currently used by the A-10 and F-15E.

The GBU-15 CWW TV-guided bomb on a 48th FW F-111F.

TYPE: EGBU-15 MODULAR GUIDED WEAPON (MGW) BOMB

Manufacturer:	Boeing (Rockwell)
Country of manufacture:	USA
Diameter:	18in (457mm)
Span:	4ft 11in (1.5m)
Length:	12ft 10in (3.91m)
Weight:	2,917lb (1,324kg)
Range:	40 miles (64km)

The EGBU-15 is the latest variant of the GBU-15, and is equipped with TV, IR and GPS guidance. The appropriate system can be selected by the Weapons Systems Operator according to the weather and threat conditions prevailing at the time.

RIGHT: A close-up of the nose of a EGBU-15 Modular Guided Weapon bomb, showing the GPS receiver.

BELOW: The EGBU-15 Modular Guided Weapon bomb.

TYPE: JOINT DIRECT ATTACK MUNITION (JDAM) BOMB

Manufacturer:	Boeing
Country of manufacture:	USA

The Boeing Joint Direct Attack Munition or JDAM comprises GPS/inertial navigation kits fitted to the free-fall 1,000lb Mk.83 and designated GBU-32, 2,000lb Mk.84 bomb or BLU-109 penetrator bombs as GBU-31 to form Precision Guided Munitions (PGM). The US Navy fit a kit to the thermal-protected BLU-110 to become the GBU-35. They were designed in response to a USAF/US Navy requirement for a reduced cost PGM that was issued in the late 1980s.

The JDAM can provide accurate bombing capability in all weather conditions, by day and by

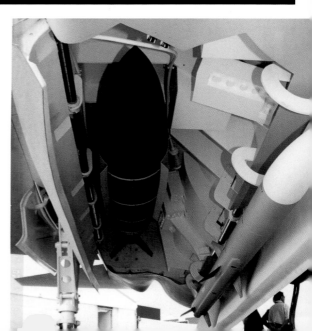

A mock-up of the Lockheed Martin X-35 Joint Strike Fighter, showing a GBU-31 JDAM with an AIM-120 AMRAAM in the weapons bay.

night. The JDAM is continually updated with target information through the aircraft avionics and once released will use its INS navigation to guide it on to the target. The GPS periodically checks the position and provides correction data in flight if required.

Further improvements to JDAM requested by the US Navy may include a terminal seeker which could further improve the accuracy. An extended range JDAM has been demonstrated using the Alenia Marconi Diamond Back kit (see separate entry) which can extend the range from 28km to 110km (17–68 miles).

The USAF have also shown interest in a kit to be fitted to existing 500lb and 250lb bombs, and a GBU-38 has been built with the Mk.82 for trials.

JDAM has been cleared for use with B-1B, B-2, B-52H, F-15E, F-16, F/A-18 and others will follow. It is in service with the USAF and USN and was used operationally against Serb targets with great success from B-2s, with over 650 being dropped. Interest is being shown from a number of countries for use with the air arms.

GBU-31, 2,000lb Joint Direct Attack Munition (JDAM) Bomb

Manufacturer:	Boeing
Country of manufacture:	USA
Diameter:	18in (457mm)
Length:	12ft 8in (3.86m)
Weight:	2,060lb (935kg)

The GBU-31 JDAM can be based on the 2,000lb BLU-109 penetrator bomb...

...or a standard 2,000lb Mk.84 bomb.

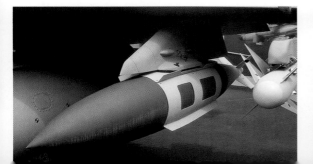

GBU-32, 1,000lb Joint Direct Attack Munition (JDAM) Bomb

Manufacturer:	Boeing
Country of manufacture:	USA
Diameter:	4in (356mm)
Length:	10ft (3.05m)
Weight:	1,030lb (468kg)

The GBU-32 JDAM uses the 1,000lb Mk.83 bomb.

GBU-35, 1,000 Joint Direct Attack Munition (JDAM) Bomb

Manufacturer:	Boeing
Country of manufacture:	USA
Diameter:	14in (356mm)
Length:	10ft (3.05m)
Weight:	1,030lb (468kg)

The GBU-35 JDAM is unique to the US Navy and uses the 1,000 BLU-110 bomb which has a thermal coating for increased safety for use aboard ships.

GBU-38, 500lb Joint Direct Attack Munition (JDAM) Bomb

Manufacturer:	Boeing
Country of manufacture:	USA

The GBU-38 JDAM uses the 500lb Mk.82 general purpose bomb and had been developed in response to USAF interest in having kits to fit to their smaller bombs.

Currently under trial is the GBU-38 JDAM, which uses the 500lb Mk.82 general purpose bomb.

Boeing are also looking at a kit for the 250lb Mk 81 bomb for the USAF. Further improvements to JDAM requested by the US Navy may include a terminal seeker which could further improve taccuracy. An extended range JDAM has been demonstrated using the Alenia Marconi Diamond Back kit (see separate entry), which can extend the range from 28km to 110km (17–68 miles).

During Operation *Allied Force* over 650 JDAMs were dropped by the B-2 Spirit stealth bomber.

TYPE: HAVE LITE (POPEYE 2) MISSILE

Manufacturer:	PGSUS (Rafael/Lockheed Martin)
Country of manufacture:	USA
Diameter:	21in (530mm)
Span:	5ft (1.52m)
Length:	13ft 11in (4.24m)
Weight:	2,500lb (1,135kg)

The Have Nap is similar to the AGM-142 Have Nap, but has been built for lighter aircraft such as the F-16 Fighting Falcon.

The Have Lite is an advanced air-to-ground precision guided missile developed by PGSUS (a Lockheed Martin/Rafael joint venture) from the AGM-142 Have Nap/Popeye missile. It is approximately 500lb (227kg) lighter than the AGM-142, but retains its features. It has been designed to enable smaller single-seat aircraft such as the F-16, Mirage 2000 and Kfir to operate the missile.

The Have Lite can be operated in a variety of mission profiles, and with its significant stand-off range it minimizes fighter aircraft exposure to heavily defended targets. It can be programmed to fly low- or high-level horizontal profiles as well as vertical trajectories. It incorporates autonomous mid-course, guidance-based on GPS-aided inertial navigation. The missile then homes in on the target using a high-performance IIR or TV seeker and accurately delivers either a penetration or blast fragmentation warhead. It is powered by a solid-fuel rocket motor which burns out well before reaching the target, thus providing a low noise and IR signature which makes it more difficult to detect and destroy. It can be armed with a 341kg (750lb) general purpose or a 364kg (800lb) penetrator warhead, which it can deliver to within 3m (10ft) of the target.

TYPE: HOT MISSILE

Manufacturer:	MBDA (Euromissile)
Country of manufacture:	France/Germany
Diameter:	5.9in (150mm)
Span:	12.2in (310mm)
Length:	4.27ft (1.3m)
Weight:	71.6lb (32.5kg)
Range:	2.7 miles (4.3km)

The HOT (*Hautsubsonique Optiquement téléguidé tiré d'un Tube*) anti-tank missile is a European international collaboration programme initiated in 1964 by Nord in France and Bölkow in Germany for their respective armed forces. Euromissile was established to manage the project and quantity production commenced in 1977 for use from armoured vehicles.

The helicopter-mounted version of the HOT missile was developed at the same time and initially entered service with the French Army in 1980. The HOT missile remains sealed in a glass-fibre tube throughout its life and only emerges when fired. Target acquisition is through a roof-mounted stabilized sight and once in flight the missile is controlled via a trailed cable down which flight control instructions are transmitted. Deviations from the required flight are automatically calculated and instructions from the command computer are made to the missile exhaust deflectors, which bring it back to the line of sight.

HOT development continued and in 1985 production of the HOT 2 commenced, featuring an improved warhead in an enlarged diameter missile. Development continued with HOT 3, which has a tandem warhead and can defeat reactive armament. It entered service in 1993.

HOT was initially built for use with the German Army Bo105 helicopter and the French Army SA342 Gazelle, but can also be used with the Dauphin/Panther, Lynx and Tiger. As with these helicopters that were widely exported, the HOT missiles have also seen considerable export success, especially in the Middle East. Within NATO HOT is used by France, Germany and Spain.

RIGHT: A pair of HOT anti-tank missile launcher tubes on a French Army Gazelle.

TYPE: KEPD 150, KEPD 350/TAURUS (MAW) DISPENSER MISSILE

Manufacturer:	Taurus Systems
Country of manufacture:	Germany
Span:	24.8in (630mm)
Length:	16.4ft (5m)
Height:	12.6in (320m)
Weight:	3,086lb (1,400kg)
Range:	217 miles (350km)

The KEPD 150 and 350 (Kinetic Energy Penetrator and Destroyer) and Taurus 350 are a family of long-range weapons currently under final development for the German and Swedish Armed forces.

The KEPD 150 has a 150km (93-mile) range and the KEPD 350 – 350km (218 miles). Both are armed with a 450kg warhead which can be either armour-piercing or high-explosive. The Taurus 350 has a 300km (186-mile) range and can be fitted with the same warhead or submunitions. All have an INS/GPS combined with terrain navigation system and use an imaging IR seeker for target recognition during the final stage of the attack.

It is planned that the German Air Force will be taking a quantity of the KEPD 350 for use with their Tornado and later with the Typhoon. Sweden plans to use the KEPD 120 with their Gripen.

ABOVE: The Taurus KEPD 150.

BELOW: The Taurus KEPD 350.

AIR-TO-GROUND WEAPONS

73

KH-29TE (AS-14 'KEDGE') MISSILE

Manufacturer:	Vympel
Country of manufacture:	Russia/USSR
Diameter:	15.75in (400mm)
Span:	3.61ft (1.1m)
Length:	12.8ft (3.90m)
Weight:	1,521lb (690kg)
Range:	18.6 miles (30km)

The Kh-29 is understood to have been developed during the 1970s and entered service the following decade. It has been allocated the NATO reporting designation of AS-14 'Kedge' and is a laser- or TV-guided air-to-ground missile.

The three models of the Kh-29 are known to exist. These are the Kh-29L which is laser designated and has a launch weight of 660kg (1,455lb) and a range of up to 10km (6 miles). The Kh-29T is TV-guided, providing a TV image to the aircraft via a data link and enabling the crew to guide the missile on to the target. This model has a launch weight of 680kg (1,500lb) and a range of up to 12km (7.5 miles). The Kh-29TE is an improved version of the Kh-29T with increased weight and range. Each of the missiles is similar in size and shape, but the Kh-29L has a tapered nose while the TV-guided models have no taper.

The Kh-29TE TV-guided anti-ship missile.

Each of the missiles are armed with a high-explosive, penetration warhead and are capable of being used against concrete shelters and runways as well as bridges, while the T and TE can also be used against ships.

The Kh-29 can be carried by a number of Russian-built aircraft, including the MiG-27, MiG-29, Su-24, Su-25 and Su-27. They are in service with many operators of these aircraft including the Czech, Hungarian and Polish Air Forces.

KMG-U DISPENSER

Manufacturer:	Bazalt
Country of manufacture:	Russia
Diameter:	21.46in (545mm)
Span:	18.11in (460mm)
Length:	12.14ft (3.7m)
Weight:	Up to 1,160lb (526kg)

The KMG-U (*Konteyner Malogabaritnykh Gruzov Universalnyi* or universal small-size cargo container) is a submunition container designed to carry a range of bomblets.

The KMG-U can carry between eight and 248 anti-armour or fragmentation bomblets – the overall weight of the weapon would depend on the bomblets fitted. It would appear that these bomblets are ejected from the container, which remains attached to the aircraft.

The KMG-U can be carried by most Russian attack aircraft and it is in service with many of the former Warsaw Pact air forces.

The KMG-U submunition dispenser.

Manufacturer:	Lockheed Martin
Country of manufacture:	USA
Diameter:	4in (101mm)
Span:	13in (330mm)
Length:	6ft 3in (1.9m)
Weight:	88.85lb (40.3kg)

The Laser-Guided Training Round (LGTR) was developed by Loral to provide LGB training without having to write off the cost of complete GBU.

The LGTR uses a standard Paveway II front section, including the semi-active laser seeker. Like the GBUs, the difference between the actual trajectory and that required to hit the target is

The Laser-Guided Training Round mounted on a USMC F/A-18D Hornet.

constantly calculated and the required corrections are fed to the forward control surfaces to steer it back on track.

Lockheed Martin have also been promoting an armed LGTR named the Minimum Collateral Damage Weapon (MCDW), which could be used to hit a target that may be in a town or surrounded by civilians. Trials have taken place in the UK as well as the USA.

The LGTR has been in use with the USMC and US Navy and exports have included Canada and Spain.

Manufacturer:	Various
Country of manufacture:	Various
Diameter:	16.06in (408mm)
Span:	22.44in (570mm)
Length:	7ft 1in (2.16m)
Weight:	750lb (340kg)

The 750lb M117 general purpose blast bomb was developed in the 1960s for use with US strike and bomber aircraft, and was initially used

Twelve M117 bombs on a Heavy Stores Adapter Beam under each wing plus a further 27 in the bomb bay gives the B-52G Stratofortress an impressive warload.

AIR-TO-GROUND WEAPONS

75

The M117 was extensively used during the Gulf War when B-52s carried fifty-one of these bombs – twenty-seven internally and a further twelve on each of two pylons. During the war, the B-52G flew a total of 1,624 missions and dropped almost 26,000 tons of bombs – nearly half of the total 55,000 tons dropped by all coalition forces – and nearly 15,000 tons of these were the 750lb M117s. These were usually dropped by three aircraft formations flying at altitude, blasting an area 1.5 miles long by 1 mile wide. The ground forces would be unaware of the attack until the first of the 153 explosions occurred. Besides the destructive power, the psychological effect was also considerable. It was reported that one Iraqi battalion commander surrendered because he had seen the devastation inflicted on another similar unit.

The M117 stock must have been considerably reduced during the Gulf War, although it is probable that some remain as they are still an effective weapon.

USAF 750lb M117 bombs with graffiti messages on a B-52G Stratofortress during the Gulf War.

during the Vietnam War. It is a standard iron bomb to which a number of fuses enable airburst, impact or delay options to be selected. In addition, various tails can be fitted to provide a low-drag or high-drag capability for medium- and low-level operations.

TYPE:	MK.80 LOW-DRAG GENERAL PURPOSE BOMBS

Manufacturer: Various
Country of manufacture: Various

The development of the Mk.80 series of low-drag general purpose bombs began back in 1950s. These bombs have not only become the

standard bomb for the US armed forces but for many others as well. A number of countries have built their bombs to the same specification and with standard NATO suspension lugs, they are fully interchangeable.

There are four low-drag general purpose bombs in the Mk.80 family. The Mk.81 is the smallest at 250lb, followed by the 500lb, 1,000lb and 2,000lb. While the shell case has seen little change over the years, there has been

Armourers fitting the preparing 500lb Mk.82 bombs prior to loading into a B-1B Lancer at RAF Fairford during operations against Serb targets.

Armourers fitting the tails on to Mk.82 bombs prior to loading into a B-1B Lancer at RAF Fairford during operations against Serb targets.

a large permutation of nose, fuse, explosive filling and tails, including retarded for dropping at low level.

All four bomb types are used by the USAF, USMC and US Navy, although for a period the Mk.83 was not used by the USAF. In addition, the US Navy Mk.82 and Mk.83 bombs went through a modification process in which they were refilled with the less sensitive PBXN-109.explosive, after which they were redesignated BLU-111/B and BLU-110/B. Most US Navy bombs, especially those taken to sea, have been fitted with a thermal coating, which gives them a dimpled appearance. This is to make the bombs safer when stored aboard ships.

When used for low-level missions the Mk.80 bombs can be fitted with the Ballute retarding system. This comprises a bolt-on tail unit that appears similar to the standard conical tail. This contains an inflatable balloon parachute which is deployed to slow down the bomb during a low-level mission in order to avoid damage to the aircraft from the bomb blast. The pilot has the ability to select the deployment of the Ballute when the bomb is dropped or for it to remain in its low-drag mode. The Ballute tail can be seen on the 250 EU2 bomb.

The Mk.80 bombs frequently provide the warhead for a variety of other weapon systems such as Paveway, GBU-15, GBU-130 and the JDAM family. They have even been used to produce the Quickstrike mines.

The Mk.80 family of bombs is the standard general purpose bomb of the US and many other armed forces, although the 250lb Mk 81 is not so common. They can be found in the inventories of most operators of US-built aircraft.

Mk.81 250lb Low-Drag General Purpose Bomb

Manufacturer:	Various
Country of manufacture:	USA
Diameter:	9in (228mm)
Span:	12.6in (320mm)
Length:	6.17ft (1.88m)
Weight:	260lb (118kg)

A French Mk.81 low-drag general purpose bomb built by SAMP.

Mk.82 500lb Low-Drag General Purpose Bomb

Manufacturer:	Various
Country of manufacture:	Various
Diameter:	10.75in (273mm)
Span:	15in (380mm)
Length:	7ft 3in (2.21m)
Weight:	531lb (241kg)

500lb Mk.82 low-drag general purpose bombs on a truck – just part of the bomb load of 84 B-1B Lancer prepared and ready for another mission against Serb targets.

BELOW: The Mk.82 is the 500lb model of what has become the standard USAF family of bombs.

Mk.82 500lb Snakeye Bomb

Manufacturer:	Various
Country of manufacture:	(Spain) USA

The 500lb Snakeye bomb is a Mk.82 low-drag general purpose bomb which has been fitted with pop-out retarding fins for use in low-level missions. These Mk.82 variants have been built by the Spanish manufacturer Maarsu.

Mk.83 1,000lb Low-Drag General Purpose Bomb

Manufacturer:	Various
Country of manufacture:	Various
Diameter:	12.75in (350mm)
Span:	19in (480mm)
Length:	9ft 10in (3m)
Weight:	985lb (447kg)

A pair of 1,000lb Mk.83 low-drag general purpose bombs being prepared by armourers prior to loading on to a USMC F/A-18 Hornet. Note that the grey bomb has the thermal insulation and is designated a BLU-110/B, while the drab one does not and remains a Mk.83.

Mk.84 2,000lb Low-Drag General Purpose Bomb

Manufacturer:	Various
Country of manufacture:	Various
Diameter:	18in (460mm)
Span:	2.1ft (640mm)
Length:	12ft 7in (3.84m)
Weight:	1,971lb (894kg)

The 2,000lb low-drag general purpose bomb was originally developed in the 1950s as the standard bomb for the US armed forces. It has since become the standard 2,000lb bomb for many countries and licence production has been carried out by many.

The Mk.84 bomb is currently in service with most NATO air forces.

ABOVE: The 2,000lb Mk.84 low-drag general purpose bomb is currently in service with most NATO air forces and many others throughout the world, some of which have undertaken licence production.

BELOW: A 2,000lb Mk.84 low-drag general purpose bomb is carried by a MHU-83 loader to a B-52H Stratofortress ready for a mission against Serb targets.

TYPE:	MK.20 ROCKEYE II DISPENSER

Manufacturer:	Ferranti
Country of manufacture:	USA
Diameter:	13.19in (335mm)
Span:	2ft 9.75in (860mm)
Length:	7ft 8in (2.34m)
Weight:	511lb (232kg)

The Rockeye Mk.20 Cluster Bomb Unit (CBU) comprises the Mk.7 dispenser and the Mk.118 munitions. Developed in the early 1960s by the Naval Weapons Center, it entered service in 1968 and was used extensively in Vietnam and later during the Gulf War.

Rockeye is armed with 247 Mk.118 submunitions that have an effective capability against ships and tanks. Rockeye can be dropped from a variety of heights, which determine the area covered. Later production incorporated a sensor in the fuse which would initiate the release of the bomblets at a predetermined height.

Although developed by the US Navy, Rockeye was also ordered in substantial numbers by the USAF. A variant of the Rockeye dispenser has also been ordered by the US Navy as the Mk.6. This dispenser has a thermal coating and additional internal safety features to protect it from any fire aboard ship.

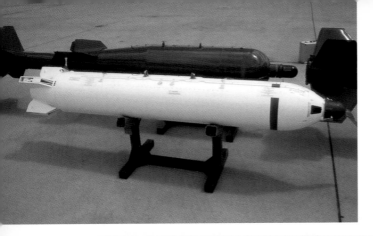

Rockeye remains in service with the USAF and US Navy as well as a number of other NATO countries including Denmark, the Netherlands, Norway and Turkey. It is a dumb weapon, needing no connection with the aircraft weapon system, and it is therefore compatible with most US tactical aircraft including the F-16, which is operated by all of these countries.

The Rockeye cluster bomb was widely used during the Gulf War.

TYPE: MW-1 MULTI-PURPOSE WEAPON

Manufacturer:	LFK/RTG
Country of manufacture:	Germany
Diameter:	4.33ft (1.32m)
Length:	17.49ft (5.33m)
Height:	2.13ft (650mm)
Weight:	10,361lb (4,700kg)

The multi-purpose weapon MW-1 (*Mehrzweckwaffe*) was developed by Raketen Technik in the mid 1960s as a submunition dispensing weapon.

The MW-1 was developed to overcome the shortcomings of the current and envisaged CBUs, which had set submunition loads and distribution patterns. MW-1 could be loaded with various submunitions and had an easily modifiable distribution pattern. The dispenser has 112 launch tubes and each tube can carry up to forty-two bomblets.

The MW-1 was originally planned for use with the F-104G Starfighter of the German Air Force for use against armour and airfields. The MW-1 was later adopted to be a primary weapon for the German and Italian Air Force Tornados.

ABOVE: The MW-1 dispenser. Depending on the submunitions type loaded they can dispense 4,704 anti-armour bomblets.

BELOW: A German Navy Tornado IDS releases the bomblets from the MW-1 to create a devastating attack.

Manufacturer:	Bazalt
Country of manufacture:	Russia
Diameter:	15.75in (400mm)
Span:	17.72in (450mm)
Length:	7.55ft (2.3m)
Weight:	1,135lb (515kg)

The OFAB (*Oskolochno-Fugasnaya Aviatsionnaya Bomba* or fragmentation/high-explosive aircraft bomb) is a family of high-explosive bombs.

The OFAB has been built in a range of sizes, with the number part of the designation indicating the weight of the bomb. These include 100kg, 120kg, 250kg and 500kg and many of these have sub-variants for specific missions.

The OFAB bombs have been cleared to be carried by most Russian-built attack and bomber aircraft and are on the inventories of many of these countries including the Czech Republic, Hungary and Poland.

A model of the Bazalt OFAB-500U fragmentation bomb.

Manufacturer:	Elbit
Country of manufacture:	Israel
Diameter:	10.75in (273mm)
Span:	2.3ft (700mm)
Length:	11.25ft (3.43m)
Weight:	716.5lb (325kg)

The Opher terminal guidance kits were developed by Elbit in the early 1980s to attach to a standard iron bomb to make it into a PGM.

When fitted to a bomb, the Opher looks very similar to the Paveway II, but instead of using reflected laser light for the designation the head is fitted with an IR seeker. Depending on the launch profile, the PGM can be launched some 7km (4 miles) from the target and will expect to be able to spot the target at around 1km (0.6 miles). It can differentiate between a target already hit and can make adjustments for one on the move.

A later development named Whizzard incorporates recognition algorithms, enabling it to target specific vehicles.

The Opher system has been cleared for use on most Israeli Air Force aircraft and it has been exported to several countries including Italy.

The Israeli-built Elbit Opher terminal guidance kit can easily be mistaken for a Paveway II, but has an IR seeker rather than laser.

Manufacturer:	Bazalt
Country of manufacture:	Russia
Diameter:	17.8in (450mm)
Length:	8.2ft (2.5m)
Weight:	1,102lb (500kg)

ABOVE: The RBK-500U cluster bomb.

The RBK (*Razovaya Bombovaya Kasseta* or single-use bomb cassette) is a Russian-built CBU designed to carry a range of submunitions. As with many of this type of weapon, it can be fitted with a range of bomblets. These can range from anti-personnel to anti-armour.

The RBK-500 weighs around 500kg depending on the type of submunition loaded, which can include the SFW. There are also smaller RBK-250 and RBK-250 variants.

The RBK-500 is displayed here with a MiG-29, but having standard Russian mounting lugs, it can be fitted to a variety of aircraft including MiG-21, MiG-23 Su-22, Su-24, Su-25 and Su-27. These weapons are in service with Russian as well as many air forces that operate these aircraft, including those of the Czech Republic, Hungary and Poland.

RIGHT: A model of the RBK-500 SPBE-D together with one of the fifteen SPBE-D SFW it can carry. There is also a piece or armour to illustrate the capability of the weapon.

The PFM-1 bomblets can be fitted in a number of Russian CBUs.

PFM-1 Bomblet

Manufacturer:	Not known
Country of manufacture:	Russia

The PFM-1 bomblets are a submunition which can be distributed in a number of ways, including CBUs such as the RBK and PROSAB.

The PFM-1 has been nicknamed the 'Green Parrot'. It resembles a sycamore seed in flight, spinning and spreading out. It is filled with a liquid explosive and the spinning effect continues in the liquid after it has landed, triggering the arming. Any pressure on the plastic casing will cause it to explode, causing serious injury.

Manufacturer:	Various
Country of manufacture:	USA
Diameter:	17in (430mm)
Span:	1ft 11in (580mm)
Length:	7ft 7.75in (2.33m)
Weight:	Load-dependent

The SUU-30 (Suspended Underwing Unit 30) was developed during the 1960s and comprises a container which can be loaded with a variety of BLU (Bomb Live Unit) submunitions.

As a weapon, the SUU-30 does not exist, but when loaded (at the factory) with submunitions it takes the appropriate CBU designation. Being unguided and having standard mounting lugs, it is capable of being carried by most US and NATO attack aircraft. Once launched, the container splits, releasing the submunitions. The timing of the container split and the pattern of the submunitions can be preset prior to flight.

The SUU-30 dispenser has been the basis of a number of cluster bombs and each one has a CBU- designation according to the submunition.

TYPE: WCMD (WIND-CORRECTED MUNITIONS DISPENSER) KIT

Manufacturer: Lockheed Martin
Country of manufacture: USA

The WCMD is an inexpensive tail kit that turns existing cluster munitions (CBU-87/B CEM, CBU-89/B GATOR, and CBU-97/B SFW) into all-weather precision-guided weapons. By correcting for launch transients, ballistic errors and winds aloft, Lockheed Martin's WCMD provides strike aircraft with an accurate pattern lay-down capability for cluster munitions from any operational altitude or weather condition.

Now entering pilot production, the WCMD consists of an inertial measurement unit, active control surfaces, and unique wind estimation and compensation algorithms. It simply replaces the existing tail unit

A 'one kit fits all' approach with a MIL-STD-1760 interface enables compatibility with all USAF strike aircraft including B-1, B-2, B-52, F-15E, F-16 and F-117. The common retrofit kit hardware and common mission planning software are the same for all CBUs. The WCMD can be pre-programed prior to the mission or during the flight prior to launch. Each weapon can be independently targeted to achieve maximum operational effectiveness.

In an effort to keep the costs of the WCMD affordable, Lockheed Martin have produced the kit with a minimal number of parts, thus reducing the production time.

An initial production order was placed in 1997 for the WCMD and it entered service in 1999 with the USAF, who have a planned requirement for 50,000 kits.

Engineers check a trial WCMD tail kit. (Photo Lockheed Martin via API)

The tail section of the WCMD which replaces the tail of existing CBU weapons. (Photo Lockheed Martin via API)

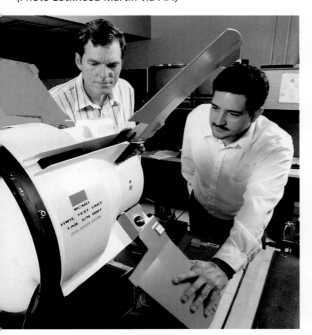

Manufacturer:	Eurotorp
Country of manufacture:	France
Diameter:	12.75in (324mm)
Length:	8.86ft (2.7m)
Weight:	487lb (221kg)
Max speed:	7kts
Range:	4.3 miles (7km)

The Eurotorp A.244 lightweight torpedo was originally developed by Whitehead Moto Fides of Italy in the 1960s to replace the US-designed Mk.44 for Italian Navy use in the shallow waters of the Mediterranean. It entered service in 1971.

The A.244S is an improved model with a new seeker which entered service with the Italian Navy in the early 1980s. A Mod 1 emerged a couple of years later with a further improved seeker.

The A.244S has been cleared for use by a number of helicopters and aircraft such as the AB-

An A.244S Mod 1 lightweight torpedo.

212, SH-3D, EH-101 and Enforcer. It is in service with a number of countries including Greece, Italy and Turkey.

Manufacturer:	Boeing (McDonnell Douglas)
Country of manufacture:	USA
Diameter:	13.5in (330mm)
Span:	3ft (914mm)
Length:	12ft 7.5in (3.84m)
Weight:	1,145lb (520kg)
Range:	57+ miles (92km)

The AGM-64 Harpoon anti-ship missile was developed by McDonnell Douglas in the early 1970s as an air-launched missile for use by the US Navy to attack boats, ships and submarines. Harpoon was first launched in 1972, and about the same time the US Navy expanded the requirement to include a ship-launched model, followed by a further requirement for a submarine-launched model a year later.

In 1973 the Harpoon was selected as the prime ASV weapon for the US Navy and it was designated AGM-84A for the air-launched model, RGM-84A for the ship-launched and UGM-84A for submarine-launched. Deliveries to the US Navy commenced in 1977.

Various upgrades have been introduced, commencing with the Block 1B in 1982 which featured an advanced guidance system developed for the Royal Navy. The Block 1B flies towards its target at even lower altitudes, making detection and defence by a target ship more difficult. A further enhanced Block 1C began delivery in 1984 as the AGM-84C for

the US Navy and the AGM-84D for the USAF. The AGM-84D had also been modified for use by the conventional-armed B-52H, which can carry eight to twelve missiles depending on the configuration.

The Block 1D Harpoon was designed with new software and guidance system which would be available in a retrofit kit. Complete with an increased range, this would enable the missile to re-attack a target by flying cloverleaf-shaped search patterns. Plans for the Harpoon Block 1D upgrade were abandoned after the collapse of the former Soviet Union. However, the re-attack capability and improved guidance were incorporated in the new Block 1G variant, and when flight testing was successfully completed in 1997 deliveries to international customers commenced as the AGM-84G.

The AGM-84E Stand-off Land Attack Missile (SLAM) was developed from the standard Harpoon in just twenty-seven months as an interim weapon while the AGM-137 was to be developed. However, the AGM-137 was cancelled before completion. The SLAM was fitted with the IIR seeker from the AGM-65D Maverick as well as a GPS. It also featured a data link to enable the seeker's images to be transmitted and command instructions to be received. It entered service in 1990 and saw limited action during the Gulf War.

The AGM-84H SLAM-ER is a further development of the Harpoon and is described below.

The AGM-84J Harpoon Block 2 or Harpoon 2000 is a low cost/low risk missile with expanded capability to include strikes against land-based targets. This has been achieved by utilizing the integrated GPS/INS from the JDAM and the software, mission computer and the GPS antenna and receiver from the Stand-off Land Attack Missile-Expanded Response (SLAM-ER). It can be launched from aircraft as well as surface ships, submarines or land positions.

The AGM-64 Harpoon has been approved for use with B-52, F-16, F/A-18, Nimrod, P-3 and S-3, and is in service with twenty-five international customers.

A captive CATM-84E variant of the AGM-84 on a US Navy P-3C Orion and used for training purposes.

TYPE: AGM-84H SLAM-ER MISSILE

Manufacturer:	Boeing (McDonnell Douglas)
Country of manufacture:	USA
Diameter:	13.5in (343mm)
Span:	7ft 2in (2.18m)
Length:	14ft 4in (4.37m)
Weight:	1,400lb (635kg)
Range:	174 miles (280km)

The AGM-84H SLAM-ER.

The AGM-84H SLAM-ER (Stand-off Land Attack Missile-Expanded Response) was developed following operational experience with the AGM-84E SLAM that was used during the Gulf War. Although the SLAM-ER features a 318kg (700lb)HE penetration warhead compared to the SLAM's 222kg (490lb), the 130mm (5in) shorter SLAM-ER with the folding wing enables the range to be extended from 95km to 280km (60–174 miles). The SLAM-ER also features improved navigation with automated mission planning.

The US Navy has a requirement for 600 AGM-84H SLAM-ERs and production of the first batch is under way.

Future developments include the SLAM-ER Plus with automatic target recognition, although operator assistance will remain available. A 1,089kg (2,400lb) enlarged Grand SLAM has also been proposed with improved navigation and data link, larger warhead and fuel capacity for a 300km (186-mile) range.

TYPE: AGM-119 PENGUIN MISSILE

Manufacturer:	Kongsberg
Country of manufacture:	Norway
Diameter:	11in (280mm)
Span:	4.59ft (1.4m)
Length:	10.5ft (3.2m)
Weight:	815lb (370kg)
Max speed:	High subsonic
Range:	34 miles+ (55km+)

The Penguin 3 is a development of the Kongsberg anti-ship missile specifically for use by fixed-wing aircraft. It has evolved from the ship-launched Penguin 1 with a new, fully digitized guidance system and has been developed for use by Norwegian Air Force F-16s. This variant of the Penguin missile started its development at the end of the 1970s – prior to the helicopter-launched Penguin 2 Mod 7, hence its apparent out-of-sequence designation AGM-119A. Although developed for the F-16, Penguin 3 is capable of being carried by other aircraft and integration with the Eurofighter Typoon will take place soon. The F-16 can carry a weapon load of four Penguin 3s and four AIM-9 Sidewinder missiles.

The AGM-119 Penguin 2 Mod.7 with wings folded for carriage by helicopter.

The air launch of a Penguin missile commenced after the input of way points and target position either during or prior to the mission. Once launched, the missile is completely autonomous, leaving the aircraft able to mount another attack or return to base. The missile will fly the designated route using a very accurate inertial navigation system and as it approaches the target area it will use its high-resolution passive seeker for target recognition. Because the system recognizes the target it is resistant to any countermeasures that may be used. As the missile approaches the target it will drop down to a low-level height and aim to hit just above the water line.

The normal attack mission adopted by the Norwegian Air Force is to fire several Penguin missiles and time them to hit the target simultaneously. An alternative feature that can be programmed into the Penguin when there are multiple targets is that it can detect when its target has already been hit, fly over it, then locate and attack an alternative target. In this way, a number of missiles can be allocated to the highest value target and, once destroyed, deal with lesser targets all in the same attack.

Delivery of the Penguin 3 to the Norwegian Air Force commenced in 1987 and they are currently the only operator of this missile.

The Penguin 2 Mod 7 was developed from the air-launched Penguin 3, with the capability of being launched from helicopters. Work on this model of the missile commenced in the mid 1980s, in co-operation with Grumman. It attracted interest from the US Navy. Consequently, it was allocated the US designation AGM-119. As development of this helicopter-launched variant commenced after the Penguin 3 it was designated the B model. Trials progressed to integrate the missile with the SH-60B Seahawk, and these have been successfully completed.

The operation of the Penguin 2 Mod 7 is similar to the Penguin 3. The main differences are that this model is fitted with a booster motor to enable it to get from helicopter speed to its high subsonic cruise, which would not be required when launched from a fixed-wing aircraft. It is also fitted with folded wings, which reduce its wingspan to 560mm (22in) to enable it to be easily attached to a helicopter. At 3m (9.8ft) long, this model is slightly shorter than the Mk.3, but it is also a little heavier at 385kg (850lb) and therefore has a shorter range at 34km (20 miles) plus.

The Penguin 2 Mod 7 has been supplied to the Greek, Turkish and US Navies for use with the SH-60/SH-70, and a further order has been received from the Australian Navy to operate with their SH-2s. The Spanish Navy is also interested in the Penguin to arm the AV-8B Harriers and their SH-60Bs.

Four Penguin 3 anti-ship missiles ready for loading on to a Norwegian Air Force F-16A Fighting Falcon. (Photo Mediafoto via API)

Manufacturer:	NAWC
Country of manufacture:	USA
Diameter:	14in (356mm)
Span:	5.25ft (1.6m)
Length:	14ft 2.5in (4.33m)
Weight:	1,282lb (582kg)
Range:	4.3 miles (7 km)

The AGM-123 Skipper was developed in the early 1980s to provide the US Navy with a stand-off weapon based on the successful Paveway system. Initial work was carried out by the Naval Weapons Center at China Lake. Although the Paveway LGB had proved to be an effective weapon, its range was too short for naval use when dropped at low level over the sea. A rocket motor was therefore fitted, the same one as fitted to the Shrike ARM. By using already existing components, the US Navy and Marine Corps were able have an effective weapon at a substantially lower cost than Paveway III. Although the Paveway III would have been more accurate it still would not have been able to meet the required range. As a result of the saving, the US Navy and Marine Corps were able to acquire a substantial number of the AGM-123 Skipper LGBs.

The AGM-123A Skipper is based on the GBU-16 Paveway II with the 1,000lb Mk.83 bomb. Kits have been built to modify the existing LGB into the Skipper. It has been cleared for use with the A-6 and A-7 and is now cleared to be carried by the F/A-18.

ABOVE: Four AGM-123 Skipper rocket-powered LGBs on a US Navy A-6 Intruder. Photo (Aerojet via API)

RIGHT: The rocket motor enables the AGM-123 Skipper to be launched at a safer stand-off distance than the Paveway for attacks on ships. (Photo Aerojet via API)

Manufacturer:	MBDA (Aerospatiale)
Country of manufacture:	France
Diameter:	13.78in (350mm)
Length:	15.59ft (4.69m)
Weight:	1,477lb (670kg)
Range:	31 miles (50km)

The Exocet family of anti-ship missiles was developed by Aerospatiale and entered production in 1972. It was the first Western long-range fire-and-forget anti-ship missile with sea-skimming capabilities. These missiles were first

The AM.39 Exocet air-launched variant of the anti-ship missile.

An AM.39 Exocet missile fitted to a French Air Force Mirage F.1CR plus a Durandal bomb display.

used operationally by the Argentinians during the battle over the Falkland Islands, when they were successfully fired at Royal Navy ships, sinking HMS *Sheffield* and the *Atlantic Conveyor*.

The Exocet family has variants for ship launch (MM.39), submarine launch (SM.39), as well as land launch (BC) for use from coastal batteries. There is also an air-launched (AM) model which can be fired from fixed-wing aircraft as well as helicopters.

Development of the Exocet has enabled it to take advantage of new technology, and the latest Block 2 model has a much enhanced capability. It now flies lower while the homing head transmissions are delayed until close to the target, so giving little warning of its approach. The head is capable of discrimination to ensure correct target selection. It can be fired as a ripple, with the final target approach being co-ordinated to attack the target simultaneously so as to overload the defences.

Some 3,200 Exocet missiles of all variants have been sold to thirty-two countries, and it has been launched in combat in Iran, Iraq and the Gulf War as well as the Falklands.

TYPE:	**AS.15TT MISSILE**

Manufacturer:	MBDA (*Aerospatiale*)
Country of manufacture:	France
Diameter:	7.09in (180mm)
Span:	1.74ft (530mm)
Length:	7.55ft (2.3m)
Weight:	227lb (103kg)
Max speed:	628mph (1,010km/h)
Range:	10.5 miles (17km)

mands. The missile is flown at low level until close to the target, when it then drops down to a sea-skimming height

Besides the Panther, the AS.15TT has also been cleared for use with the Dauphin and Puma and could be carried by the NH90.

An AS.15TT light anti-ship missile.

The AS.15TT is part of a family of light anti-ship missiles capable of operating from ship (MM.15), coastal battery (BC.15) or from helicopters (AS.15TT). *Aerospatiale* commenced development in the mid 1970s and it was first fired in October 1982.

The AS.15TT is a development of the previous generation wire-guided AM 10 missile, but uses a radio-command guidance. The missiles have been operated by the AS 365 Panther. This is fitted with the Agrion radar which compares the location of the target and the track of the missile to generate any required course correction com-

TYPE: AS.34 KORMORAN MISSILE

Manufacturer:	LFK/Thomson-CSF (MBB)
Country of manufacture:	France/Germany
Diameter:	13.58in (345mm)
Span:	3.28ft (1.00m)
Length:	14.44ft (4.4m)
Weight:	1,323lb (600kg)
Range:	18.6 miles (30km)

MBB began development of the AS.34 Kormoran in the mid 1960s as an anti-ship missile for the German Navy. Studies had previously been conducted by Germany and France which included a proposed AS.33 missile, but this did not proceed.

Flight trials for the Kormoran commenced in 1970 and the first deliveries began in 1977. The *Marineflieger* F-104 was the first operator of the missile, followed by the Tornado. In 1983 a development programme commenced for an improved variant designated Kormoran 2. This is externally identical, but by minaturizing the electronics more space is available internally. This has been put to good use by increasing the size of the engine and the war-

One of a pair of AS.34 Kormoran anti-ship missiles fitted to a German Navy Tornado IDS.

head, resulting in an increased overall weight of 630kg (1,390lb) and an improved range of 35km (22 miles).

The Kormoran 1 is in service with the German and Italian armed forces, while the Kormoran 2 serves with just the German Navy.

TYPE: AS.37/AJ 168 MARTEL MISSILE

Manufacturer:	MBDA (Matra/BAe)
Country of manufacture:	France/UK
Diameter:	15.75in (400mm)
Span:	3.94ft (1.2m)
Length:	13.52ft (4.12m)
Weight:	2,674lb (1,213kg)
Max speed:	Mach 1
Range:	Up to 37 miles (60km)

The Martel (Missile Anti-Radar TELevision) air-to-ground missile was designed by Matra and British Aerospace in the 1960s as a joint development for their respective countries' air forces.

The Martel was developed in two models – both utilized the same airframe apart from the nose section. The AJ 168 featured a TV-guidance system and was built by British Aerospace for the RAF Buccaneers for an anti-ship role. It had a blunt nose with a lens for the TV and was therefore a little shorter at 3.87m (12.7ft). Matra built the AS 37 anti-radar model, which featured a pointed nose housing a number of passive radar seekers that could be fitted depending on the threat. It was cleared for use with the Buccaneer, Jaguar, Mirage and Atlantic. The AS.37 was used by the RAF and French Air Force and may have been exported.

A Martel on an RAF Buccaneer. Both have been withdrawn from RAF service but may remain in service elsewhere.

The RAF withdrew the Martel in the mid 1990s and it was replaced by the Sea Eagle. It may well have been withdrawn from the French Air Force inventory as the Armat has superseded it.

MK.11 MOD 3 DEPTH CHARGE

Manufacturer:	BAe Systems
Country of manufacture:	UK
Diameter:	11in (297mm)
Length:	4ft 7in (1.4m)
Weight:	320lb (145kg)

ABOVE: A pair of inert Mk.11 Depth Charges used for training purposes.

The BAe Depth charge Mk.11 Mod 3 is a reliable and effective low-cost air-launched Anti-Submarine Warfare (ASW) weapon. It tolerates the high vibrations that are associated with helicopters, and the charge case and nose section are strengthened to withstand high-velocity water entry without distortion, making it suitable for use from both helicopter and fixed-wing aircraft.

While a torpedo is the main weapon used against submarines, there are a number of scenarios where depth charges may be both more appropriate and cheaper, especially when the target is operating near the surface or in shallow water. They can also be used as a warning shot against ships or submarines and in situations when it could be dangerous to use a torpedo, for example when friendly forces are nearby.

The Mk.11 Depth Charge is supplied in three variants: the Warshot, a live-filled weapon fitted with live fuze for operational use; Drill, an inert-filled weapon complete with an inert drill fuze which is designed for ground training in weapon preparation and handling procedures; and Practice, another inert-filled weapon but with a dummy fuze for aircraft practice drops.

The Depth Charge Mk.11 is in service with the Royal Navy and other navies worldwide.

LEFT: An inert Mk.11 Depth Charge fitted to a Royal Navy Sea King.

MK 46 LIGHTWEIGHT TORPEDO

Manufacturer:	Raytheon (Hughes)/Aerojet
Country of manufacture:	USA
Diameter:	12.6in (320mm)
Length:	8ft 6in (2.6m)
Weight:	509lb (231kg)
Max speed:	45kts
Range:	7 miles (11km)

Development of the Mk.46 lightweight torpedo was begun in the latter 1950s by Aerojet to replace the Mk.44, which was unable to meet the threat of the newer, faster submarines that were also capable of diving deeper.

The Mk 46 torpedo was capable of substantially increasing its speed over that of the Mk.44. It was produced in a number models as improvements were introduced and has now reached the Mod 5. Mod 1 included changing the propulsion system from a solid fuel to a liquid fuel. Mod 2 improvements incorporated modifications to the helicopter attack system and resulted in most Mod 1 torpedoes being upgraded. Mod 3 did not enter production. Mod 4 was used to provide the armament of the Mk 60 Captor mine, which was moored in areas of suspected submarine activity. When a submarine was detected the torpedo would be fired. It featured a new, improved transducer seeker, together with an improved guidance and control computer. It was also fitted with a two-stage motor which used the lower speed during the searching sequence and then accelerated for the attack, which could double its range. A number of the Mod 2 were upgraded. The Mod 5 is also referred to as NEARTIP (NEAR Term Improvement Programme), as it was intended to fill the gap until the introduction of the Mk.50 Barracuda. Although no new torpedoes have been manufactured for some time, Raytheon continue to market refurbished surplus Mk.46s.

The Mk.46 torpedo was cleared to operate with Atlantic, AS.212, CASA 212 and 235, Fokker 50, P-3, S-70 SH-2G, US SH-3 and British Sea Kings. It has been widely exported and may remain in service with the air forces and navies of Canada, France, Germany, Greece, Italy, Norway, Portugal, Spain and Turkey, as well as the USA.

The Mk.46 lightweight torpedo remains in widespread use around the world.

TYPE: Mk 52, 55, 56 AND 57 MINES

Manufacturer:	Not known
Country of manufacture:	USA
Weight:	1,000lb (454kg)

The Mk.50 series of mines began development in the 1950s as ground mines for use against ships and submarines. They were extensively used during the Vietnam War. These mines were fitted with a range of detection systems, but they have now been superseded for operational use; some have been modified for training.

The explosive charge of the Actuation mine Mk.52 has been removed and replaced with concrete to maintain its buoyancy together with some instrumentation. A coil in the mine detects magnetic stimuli, while a hydrophone responds to any acoustic sounds. The firing mechanism has also been removed and replaced with a pyrotechnic device, which automatically surfaces to create coloured smoke to indicate that the mine has been actuated. Should the mine not be activated within a preset time, a float is released which enables the mine to be recovered without having to use divers.

Three models of the Mk.52 exist. OA-03B is fitted with a Mk.10 or 20 tail. The OA-06B has a nose and tail Mk.19 – both are fitted with a parachute. The third is the OA-05E, which is the basic mine laid by a ship. They are normally painted white with orange stripes.

The Mk.52 mine can be dropped from a B-52H, P-3C and the F/A-18, as well as being deployed by a ship.

Actuation Mine Mk 52s loaded into the bomb bay of a B-52 ready for an exercise.

Manufacturer:	Aerojet
Country of manufacture:	USA
Diameter:	20.98in (533mm)
Length:	10ft 8in (3.25m)
Weight:	2,002lb (908kg)

The Mk.62, Mk.63 and Mk.64 Quickstrike shallow water mines were developed by Aerojet from the Mk.82, Mk.83 and Mk.84 bombs. Only the Mk.65 was specially developed as a mine.

The Quickstrike mines replaced the Mk.36, Mk.40 and Mk.41 DST, which were also converted from bombs for use during the Vietnam War. When the war ended the US agreed to supply the fusing details to the Vietnamese for EOD purposes, and as a result new mechanisms were required. The Quickstrike mines also replaced the Mk.50 series of mines, as their fusing details were also supplied to the Vietnamese.

Due to their standard lug fitting, the Quickstrike mines can be carried by most US combat aircraft including the B-1 and B-52, as well as the F-14, F/A-18 and P-3 aircraft.

The US Quickstrike mines in production with Aerojet.

TYPE: Marte 2/A Missile

Manufacturer:	MBDA (Alenia Marconi (Otomelara)
Country of manufacture:	Italy
Diameter:	12.6in (320mm)
Span:	3.22ft (980mm)
Length:	12.5ft (3.78m)
Weight:	595lb (270kg)
Range:	15.5 miles+ (25km+)

Sistel began development of the Marte air-to-ground missile in the late 1960s. The development process was somewhat protracted, and it was 1977 before the missile entered production.

The Marte Mk.2A anti-ship missile.

The Marte 2 anti-ship missile was developed in the 1980s, and it is capable of being fired from ships (2/N), as well as helicopters (2/S) and light combat aircraft (2/A) such as the AMX. The helicopter model is fitted with a booster motor to enable it to accelerate quickly to speed. This has increased the length of this model to 4.8m (16ft). The Marte 2 is a fire-and-forget missile which automatically flies towards the target using information given to it at launch. During the final stage of the attack the active radar is switched on to provide a lock-on to the target prior to impact.

Marte 2 is currently in service with the Italian Navy, fitted to their SH-3D, and is also being cleared for use with the NH-90 and EH.101.

TYPE: SEA EAGLE MISSILE

Manufacturer:	MBDA (BAe)
Country of manufacture:	UK
Diameter:	15.75in (400mm)
Span:	3.94ft (1.2m)
Length:	13.6ft (4.14m)
Weight:	1,323lb (600kg)
Max speed:	Mach 0.85
Range:	68 miles (110km)

The Sea Eagle anti-ship missile was developed by British Aerospace as a replacement for the Martel during late 1970s. It entered service in the mid 1980s.

The Sea Eagle continues to use the airframe design from the Martel, but features an air intake on its belly as it is powered by a turbofan engine instead of the solid motor of the earlier design. It has a sea-skimming capability and uses an intertial navigation system and an active pulse radar, which is activated for the final stage of the attack. It is armed with a 230kg (507lb) armour-piercing, delayed-action fuzed warhead, ensuring that it explodes inside the ship. Sea Eagle is currently receiving an extensive upgrade, which will significantly improve its capabilities and ensure its effectiveness for many years to come.

The Sea Eagle was initially carried by RAF Buccaneers and Royal Navy Sea Harriers. It is now also carried by the Tornado. A helicopter-launched variant with booster motors was developed for India to be launched from its Sea Kings.

A Sea Eagle anti-ship missile on a Royal Navy Sea Harrier, which is also armed with AIM-9L Sidewinders for self-protection.

Manufacturer:	MBDA (Matra/BAe Dynamics
Country of manufacture:	UK
Diameter:	9.84in (250mm)
Span:	2.36ft (0.72m)
Length:	8.2ft (2.5m)
Weight:	324lb (147kg)
Range:	9 miles+ (15km+)

Sea Skua was originally developed by British Aerospace as an anti-ship missile in the mid 1970s, and it is capable of being used from either ship or helicopter. Although it was then still under trial, a number of missiles were taken to the South Atlantic for use during Operation Corporate in the Falklands Islands. Two attacks by Royal Navy Lynx helicopters, each using a pair of ripple-fired Sea Skua missiles, resulted in the sinking and crippling of Argentinian warships despite atrocious weather conditions. During the Gulf War a total of fifteen Iraqi vessels were sunk or severely damaged by these missiles.

Prior to launch, the target is illuminated by the helicopter's radar and the missile automatically locks on. Once launched, the missile sea-skims at high subsonic speed, until at a predetermined distance from the target it rises to target acquisition height, before hitting the target.

Besides those of the Royal Navy, the Sea Skua is carried by the Lynx, currently in service with various navies, and it is also carried by the German Navy Sea Kings and Turkish Navy AB-212s.

A Sea Skua anti-ship missile mounted on a Royal Navy Lynx.

TYPE: STING RAY LIGHTWEIGHT TORPEDO

Manufacturer:	MBDA (BAe/Marconi)
Country of manufacture:	UK
Diameter:	13.94in (354mm)
Length:	8.53ft (2.6m)
Weight:	584lb (265kg)
Max speed:	40+ kts

Development of the Sting Ray light torpedo was begun in the mid 1970s by Marconi, to produce an air-launched weapon capable of homing in on a submarine either in shallow or deep water.

ABOVE: *Sting Ray missiles fitted in the bomb bay of an RAF Nimrod maritime patrol aircraft. (Photo BAe Systems via API)*

Sting Ray entered service with the British armed forces in 1985 and it became the first torpedo to use a shaped-charge warhead. Basically similar to that used against tanks, the shaped charge produces a directional jet of molten copper to penetrate the pressure hull. In the mid 1990s an improved model emerged. The original models were referred to as Mod 0, while the improved one became the Mod 1. Externally, the two are similar, but improvements include the sensitivity of the front-end array, autopilot, inertial measurements, as well as a new digital signal processor.

Sting Ray is in service with the RAF Nimrod and Royal Navy Lynx, Merlin and Sea King. Export customers include the Norwegian Air Force.

The Sting Ray torpedo on a handling trolley. Next to it and on the Royal Navy Lynx helicopter behind are Sea Skua missiles. These two weapons are the main armoury of the Lynx, although others are also carried.

TYPE:	STONEFISH MINE

Manufacturer:	BAe Systems (GEC Marconi)
Country of manufacture:	UK
Diameter:	1.75in (533mm)
Length:	8.2ft (2.5m)
Weight:	2,183lb (990kg)

The Stonefish naval mine was developed by Marconi Underwater Systems in the late 1980s to be effective against submarines and ships. These mines can be laid by aircraft as well as submarines and ships. Being of a modular construction, the warstock variant can be assembled with several warhead sections, arming it with from 100 to 600kg (220–1,320lb) of explosive according to the requirement.

A smaller inert exercise variant of Stonefish (1.9m long) is used to provide realistic training for minehunting and minesweeping operations, and can provide a post-exercise breakdown on the effectiveness of the participants. Once the exercise has been completed, the exercise mine can be given a signal whereby it will automatically return to the surface for recovery. After a quick refurbishment it can then be reused.

ABOVE: The Stonefish can be air-dropped from a C-130 Hercules. (Photo BAE Systems via API)

RIGHT: The 100kg and 300kg warhead modules of the Stonefish mine.

An assessment and a training variant of Stonefish have also been built.

The Stonefish is in service with the British armed forces and can be dropped from Hercules or Nimrod as well from ships, and it has also been supplied to other countries.

Manufacturer:	SAT & NAWC
Country of Manufacture:	USA
Diameter:	10in (254mm)
Span:	3ft 8.5in (1.13m)
Length:	13ft 8.5in (4.18m)
Weight:	807lb (366kg)
Max speed:	Mach 2+
Range:	11.5 miles (18.5km)

The Advanced Anti-Radar Guided Missile (AARGM) is a being developed by Naval Air Systems Command and Science and Applied Technology Inc. as a systems upgrade for the AGM-88 HARM.

AARGM features a multi-sensor fuzed seeker which incorporates an advanced wideband passive Anti-Radiation Homing (ARH) seeker, INS/GPS and an active MMW seeker for terminal guidance. This will also be able to discriminate between actual targets and reflected emissions and will be able to continue the attack even after the emitter has been shut down. AARGM will provide a 'hard-kill' capability for the US Navy against current and future surface-to-air threats.

AARGM has been fitted into and tested in an AGM-88 HARM airframe, with the first firing taking place in March 2000. Initial production will be to provide in the region of 1,700 retrofit kits for the US Navy when production commences in 2006. A similar shaped-seeker section will be used, and, as a result, the AARGM will be virtually indistinguishable from the current AGM-88.

However, the AARGM seeker has been designed so that it can be easily fitted into other missile systems as small as 7in (18cm) in diameter. The model illustrated is a conceptual design for the next generation long-range missile. This will be powered by a ramjet propulsion system and will provide AARGM with greater speed, longer range and improved terminal manoeuvrability. In addition, the new missile can be carried internally in future stealth aircraft. It is reported that this model of the AARGM will have a range of 185km (115 miles) and will fly at Mach 4.

The AARGM will initially be fitted to the existing HARM missile, but a new, improved long-range missile is being developed to accommodate it.

Manufacturer:	SAGEM
Country of Manufacture:	France
Length:	9.84ft (3m)
Weight:	750lb (340kg)
Range:	Up to 37.3 miles (60km)

The Armament Air–Sol Modulaire (AASM) is a modular kit being developed by SAGEM to be fitted to a range of bombs in service with the French Air Force and Navy. The AASM will complement the Apache, which will be used to attack heavily defended in-depth, high-value targets, while the AASM will be used to attack battlefield targets such as tanks and SAM batteries. It will also augment stocks of the AS 30L.

Initially, the AASM contract is for 3,000 kits for the 250kg bomb – these can be the standard Mk.82 or the naval insensitive BLU-111

and CBEM bombs. This quantity has been split into two variants – the 'all-weather 10-metre class', which is fitted with an inertial measuring unit plus GPS. The other model is the 'day/night metre class', which also has an infrared seeker. Other variants are anticipated to include 'all-weather metre class', anti-radar and submunitions. as well as 400 to 1,000kg penetration bombs.

The AASM will be cleared for use with the Mirage 2000D and Rafale and will be used by the French Air Force and Navy. However, the aircraft connections will be standard NATO attachments and so it may well be exported once deliveries commence in 2005.

The SAGEM AASM variants will use either INS/GPS navigation or an infrared seeker to hit the target.

TYPE: ANF MISSILE

Manufacturer:	Aerospatiale Matra
Country of Manufacture:	France
Length:	19ft (5.8m)
Max speed:	Mach 2.5
Range:	93 miles+ (150km+)

The *Anti-Navire Futur* (ANF) is the latest in a series of development programmes aimed at producing a new generation of anti-ship missile to replace the Exocet.

The design for the ANF is optimized for the anti-ship role and incorporates an active radar terminal seeker, but it is possible that it will have a land-attack capability added later. It will be powered by a ramjet, which has already been built and tested in the Vesta programme. The ANF is planned to enter service in 2005.

The ANF is being developed to replace the Exocet.

TYPE: ARMIGER MISSILE

Manufacturer:	BGT
Country of Manufacture:	Germany
Diameter:	7.8in (200mm)
Length:	12ft 9.5in (4.00m)
Weight:	485lb (220kg)
Max speed:	Mach 2–3
Range:	124 miles (200km)

The Armiger is an advanced technology anti-radiation missile which uses a combination of GPS/INS as well as an RF/IIR seeker to locate radar transmissions. It can complete its attack without any further transmissions. Original development was a French/German project named Aramis, but following the withdrawal of France the project

was continued by BGT. The name changed to ARMIGER (Anti-Radiation Missile and Intelligent Guidance and Extended Range).

With a CEM of just 1m, it is designed so that it can make pinpoint attacks on SAM-site radar installations even in built-up areas without causing collateral damage to nearby residential locations. In the past, these installations have proved difficult to target due to the likelihood of civilian casualties. In addition, because of the accuracy of the missile a smaller warhead can be used to achieve the same destruction capability. The missile is therefore smaller than many earlier ARM missiles, enabling more to be carried.

ARMIGER is planned to replace the AGM-88 HARM missiles carried by the German Air Force on

their Tornado ECRs. Because of their lighter weight, four ARMIGER can be fitted in place of the two HARM currently carried.

The Armiger combines the RF/IIR seeker with the GPS/INS to attack radar sites accurately at ranges of around 100km.

TYPE: ATGW-3LR TRIGAT MISSILE

Manufacturer:	Euromissile/Daimler-Benz
Country of Manufacture:	France/Germany
Diameter:	6.26in (159mm)
Span:	16.93in (430mm)
Length:	5.25ft (1.6m)
Weight:	108lb (49kg)
Range:	3.1 miles (5km)

As its name says, the TRIGAT is a *TRoisiéme* Generation Anti-Tank missile. Initial development began in the mid 1970s with France, Germany and the UK collaborating to build a new anti-tank missile to replace each of their current weapons – these being the Milan, HOT,

Swingfire as well as the TOW. To achieve this, three variants of the new missile were proposed. These comprised the ATGW-3MR TRI-GAT, which was a man-portable ground-launched missile, a long-range vehicle-mounted system, and the ATGW-3LW TRIGAT, which is the helicopter-mounted variant.

TRIGAT uses an imaging IR staring focal plane seeker to detect and identify the target. Initial target acquisition is by the gunner using the TV or IR mast-mounted sights in respect of TRIGAT. Once designated, the system produces an evaluation of a single-shot kill, enabling the gunner to be certain of destroying the target.

ABOVE: A model of the ATGW-3LR TRIGAT missile.

Once locked on, the missile will automatically track the target – whether static or moving. The missile can then be fired, or if there are multiple targets, up to four missiles can be locked on to their own target and then fired as a ripple.

Although successful test firings were completed. the British and French armed forces withdrew from the project. However, production is still planned to commence in 2003 for the German Army. Belgium and the Netherlands have also maintained an interest in TRIGAT.

RIGHT: A quad launcher for the ATGW-3LR TRIGAT anti-tank missile.

TYPE:	BROACH WARHEAD

Manufacturer: BAe Systems / Ro Defence
Country of Manufacture: UK

The BROACH (Bomb Royal Ordnance Augmented CHarge) is an additional warhead that has been developed by BAE Systems. When fitted to standard bombs, it enables attacks on hardened targets at low level. These would

The BROACH warhead can be fitted to many weapon systems to increase their penetrative capability and is shown here fitted to the Paveway III.

otherwise require a munition such as the BLU-109, which has to be dropped at altitude to obtain the necessary kinetic energy to achieve the same penetrative power.

BROACH uses an additional warhead which fires a jet of molten copper at the target, causing considerable damage and weakening the structure immediately prior to the impact of the main warhead. The BROACH warhead can be fitted to a number of existing bombs including the Paveway II and III LGBs.

BROACH will be used with the Apache and SCALP-EG and Storm Shadow and is being proposed for a number of other weapons.

TYPE:	DIAMOND BACK RANGE EXTENSION KIT

Manufacturer: MBDA (Alenia Marconi)
Country of Manufacture: UK

The Alenia Marconi Diamond Back is a range extension kit which began development in the mid 1990s in order to increase economically the range of unpowered PGMs. It is attached underneath the munition, with the wings remaining stowed while attached to the aircraft. Once the munition is released, the wings

Once deployed, the Diamond Back wings form an unusual but strong diamond shape that can even withstand launching at supersonic speeds.

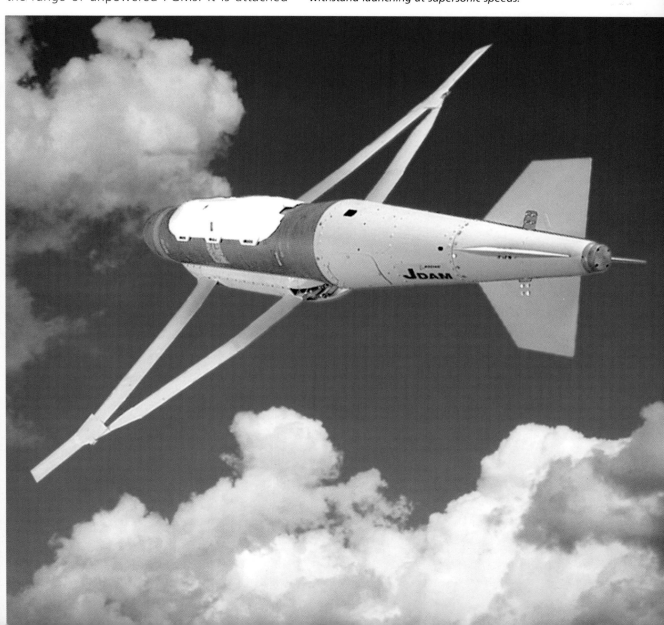

The Diamond Back fitted to JDAM during trials on a USAF F-16 Fighting Falcon.

deploy to form a diamond shape. During trials, this strap-on kit enabled a 2,000lb GBU-31 JDAM to increase its standard range from 18.5km (11.5 miles) to 65km (40 miles) when dropped from 25,000ft (7,600m) from an F-16.

It is planned to offer a range of Diamond Back kits to enable many existing and future free-fall and gliding munitions to be operated at a safer stand-off range.

TYPE:	IRIS-T MISSILE

Manufacturer:	BGT/Alenia Marconi
	(Bodenseewerk Gerätetechnik GmbH)
Country of Manufacture:	Germany/Italy/Sweden/
	Greece/Canada/Norway
Diameter:	5in (127mm)
Span:	13.78in (0.35m)
Length:	9.84ft (3.0m)
Weight:	192lb (87kg)
Range:	7.46 miles (12km)

The Germans withdrew from the ASRAAM programme. However, following reunification and evaluation of the MiG-29s and AA-11 AAMs inherited from the East German Air Force, the Germans discovered that the AA-11 missiles were superior to their existing AIM-9L. They therefore decided to instigate their own improved missile.

Referred to as the Infra-Red Improved Sidewinder-TVC or IRIS-T, this short-range, all-aspect infrared homing missile was designed by *Bodenseewerk Gerätetechnik GmbH*. They are experienced missile manufacturers, having been builders of the AIM-9 Sidewinder under licence. Like the French MICA, the IRIS-T has large fuselage wings, but to ensure compatibility with the Sidewinder, it features identical interfaces, as well as having its mass, length, diameter and centre of gravity similar to those of AIM-9L. Aerodynamic control is achieved by the tail wings and thrust vectoring. This new design enables a high off-boresight capability. This, BGT hopes, will ensure that it is attractive to current Sidewinder customers.

The commonality with the Sidewinder approach appears to have worked, as a joint MoU with Canada, Germany, Greece, Italy, Norway and Sweden was signed in 1998 for continued development and production. In addition, Denmark, the Netherlands, Portugal, Spain and Turkey are all showing interest.

The IR seeker has a +/− 90 degrees search angle, which will have an 180 degrees capability when used with a helmet-mounted sight. This has been successfully tested in a Netherlands AF F-16. Captive trials of the seeker in an AIM-9L body have proved that the IRIS-T has a superior detection and tracking capability, and live firing achieved two direct hits out of two with off-boresight angles of over 50 degrees on 25cm diameter target drones.

The IRIS-T has been designed to replace the AIM-9 Sidewinder in many NATO armed forces.

First production IRIS-T missiles are planned for delivery in 2003.

The current plans are for the IRIS-T to be cleared for use on the Tornado, Eurofighter Typhoon, JAS 39 Gripen, F-16 Fighting Falcon, CF-18 Hornet and AMX aircraft. A production of some 4,000 missiles is anticipated, with a German requirement for 2,500.

TYPE:	LONGSHOT RANGE EXTENSION AND GUIDANCE KIT

Manufacturer: Leigh Aerosystems
Country of Manufacture: USA

The Longshot is a self-contained kit that can be attached to a bomb to provide range extension and guidance.

The Longshot is attached to the weapon using the normal lug positions. It has standard NATO lugs, enabling it to be carried by most Western combat aircraft. No data bus is required, so any adjustments to the Longshot are made using a kneepad device and transmitted over the radio. The data can also be adjusted the same way by a controller on the ground.

The Longshot is another range extension kit to be fitted on to munitions – in this case, the CBU-97/B – which is also being evaluated.

Manufacturer:	MBDA (Matra BAe Dynamics)
Country of Manufacture:	International
Length:	12ft (3.65m)
Weight:	430lb (195kg)
Max speed:	Mach 4+
Range:	62 miles+ (100km+)

British Aerospace proposed the European Meteor to meet the RAF Staff Requirement (Air) 1239 for a Beyond Visual Range Air-to-Air Missile (BVRAAM) for the Typhoon in 1996. It was the subject of an intense competition with the Raytheon Future Medium-Range Air-to-Air Missile (FMRAAM), which was based on the AIM-120 AMRAAM. In May 2000 the Meteor was selected for the RAF and development is proceeding, with funding provided by a consortium split – UK (35 per cent), Germany (25 per cent), Italy (12 per cent), Sweden (12 per cent), France (10 per cent) and Spain (6 per cent).

The Meteor will be the new NATO BVRAAM when it enters service around 2008 and will equip the new generation fighters.

Meteor is powered by a variable flow ducted rocket ramjet, enabling a range in excess of 100km (60 miles) at over Mach 4. It will be equipped with proximity and impact fuzes and armed with a fragmentation warhead.

It is planned that the Meteor will enter service in 2008/10 and will initially be used to arm the Typhoon, JAS.39 Gripen, Mirage 2000 and Rafale, and subsequently cleared for operational use with most contemporary advanced fighters.

Manufacturer:	Kongsberg
Country of Manufacture:	Norway
Span:	4.59ft (1.4m)
Length:	13.45ft (4.1m)
Weight:	904lb (410kg)
Max speed:	High subsonic

The long-range NSM anti-ship missile can be launched from ship and ground platforms, as well helicopters such as this NH90.

The Kongsberg NSM (New Surface Missile) missile has been developed as a new anti-ship missile for the Norwegian fast patrol boats and frigates, in conjunction with Matra of France and LFK and TDW of Germany. The NSM is a long-range missile, and although initial proposals were for launch from ship and coastal battery, it has a multi-platform capability with the ability to be launched from a helicopter.

The NSM missile uses a high-resolution passive imaging infrared seeker to provide a high degree of discrimination as well as target selection, making it more effective in confined as well as open waters. The NSM also has the capability to be used against land targets. It has a low radar signature and an extreme sea-skimming ability, which will make it difficult to detect. In the case of a high-value target, multiple NSMs can be fired and their time at the target co-ordinated to saturate its defences.

The NSM is expected to enter military service around 2007.

Type:	Polyphem/TRIFOM Missile

Manufacturer:	MBDA
Country of Manufacture:	France/Germany/Italy
Length:	9.84ft (3.0m)
Weight:	319lb (145kg)
Range:	37 miles+ (60km+)

The Polyphem is a multi-purpose missile programme design to be operated from land sea or air capable of being used to attack land or sea targets or to be used as a reconnaissance drone. Initial development was by *Aerospatiale Matra* and LFK, and a technology demonstration programme began in 1994.

Polyphem is unusual in that although it has a long range – 60km – it uses a fibre-optic cable for command control as well as transmitting images in addition to making it immune to jamming.

It is not anticipated that Polyphem will enter service before 2007.

The Polyphem has been designed as a long-range, wire-guided, multi-purpose missile.

3PI Pre-Planned Product Improvement

AARGM Advanced Anti-Radar Guided Missile
AASM Armament Air–Sol Modulaire
ACM Advanced Cruise Missile
AFB Air Force Base
AFDS Autonomous Free-flight Dispenser System
AL Aircraft Launched
ALCM Air-Launched Cruise Missile
AMRAAM Advanced Medium-Range Air-to-Air Missile
ANF *Anti-Navire Futur*
APACHE *Arme Propulsée A CHarges Ejectables*
APC Armoured Personnel Carrier
AR Anti-Runway
ARH Anti-Radiation Homing
ARM Anti-Radiation Missile
ARMIGER Anti-Radiation Missile and Intelligent Guidance and Extended Range
ASEAN Association of South-East Asian Nations
ASMP *Air-Sol Moyenne Portée*
ASRAAM Advanced Short-Range Air-to-Air Missile
ASV Anti-surface vessel
ASW Anti-Submarine Warfare
AT Anti-Tank
ATAM Air-To-Air Mistral
ATASK Air-To-Air Starstreak

BAP *Bombe Accélérée de Pénétration*
BetAB *Betonoboynaya AviatsionnayaBbomba*
BGL *Bombe a Guidage Laser*
BIA Bomb Impact Assessment
BLU Bomb Live Unit
BROACH Bomb Royal Ordnance Augmented CHarge
BVR Beyond Visual Range
BVRAAM Beyond Visual Range Air-to-Air Missile

CALCM Conventional Air-Launched Cruise Missile
CBLS Carrier Bomb Light Store
CBU Cluster Bomb Unit
CEB Combined Effects Bomblet
CEM Combined Effects Munition
CRV Canadian Rocket Vehicle
CWW Cruciform Wing Weapon

EFP Explosively Formed Penetrator
EG *Emploi Général*
EOD Explosive Ordnance Demolition

FAB *Fugasnaya Avia Bomba*
FFAR Fin Folding Aircraft Rocket
FMRAAM Future Medium-Range Air-to-Air Missile

GP General Purpose
GPS Global Positioning System

HARM High-speed Anti Radiation Missile
HATCP *Helicoptère Air Trés Courtre Portée*
HEAT High Explosive Anti Tank
Hellfire Heliborne, Laser, Fire and Forget
HL Helicopter Launched
HMP Heavy Machine-gun Pod
HOT *Hautsubsonique Optiquement téléguidé tiré d'un Tube*
HTS HARM Targeting System
HVM Hyper Velocity Missile

INS Inertial Navigation System
IR Infrared
IRIS-T Infra-Red Improved Sidewinder-TVC
IRST Infra-Red Search and Track
ITALD Improved TALD

JASSM Joint Air-to-Surface Stand-off Missile
JDAM Joint Direct Attack Munition
JSF Joint Strike Fighter
JSOW Joint Stand-Off Weapon

KEPD Kinetic Energy Penetrator and Destroyer
KMG-U *Konteyner Malogabaritnykh Gruzov Universalnyi*

LANTIRN Low Altitude Navigation and Targeting Infra-Red Night
LGB Laser-Guided Bomb
LGTR Laser-Guided Training Round

MANPADS Man-Portable Air Defence System
Martel Missile Anti-Radar TELevision
MCDW Minimum Collateral Damage Weapon
MFBF Multi-Function Bomb Fuse
MGW Modular Guided Weapon
MICA *Missile d'Interception et de Combat et d'Autodéfence*
MMS Mast-Mounted Sight
MMW Milli Metric Wave
MoU Memorandum of Understanding
MW *Mehrzweckwaffe*

NATO North Atlantic Treaty Organization
NBC Nuclear, Biological and Chemical
NEARTIP NEAR Term Improvement Programme
NSM New Surface Missile
OFAB *Oskolochno-Fugasnaya Aviatsionnaya Bomba*

PGM Precision Guided Munition
PMTC Pacific Missile Test Centre
RAAF Royal Australian Air Force

RAF Royal Air Force
RAM Radar-Absorbing Material
RBK *Razovaya Bombovaya Kasseta*
RCB Runway Cratering Bomb
RDI Pulse-Doppler Radar
RMP Reprogrammable Micro-Processor
RMP Rocket Machine-gun Pod

SAL Supersonic Aircraft Launched
SAM Surface-to-Air Missile
SAR Semi-Active Radar
SCALP *Système de Croisière conventional Autonone à Longue Portée de precision*
SEAD Suppression of Enemy Air Defences
SFW Sensor-Fuzed Weapon
SHORAD SHOrt Range Air Defence
Sidearm (SIDEwinder Anti-Radiation Missile)
SLAM Stand-off Land Attack Missile
SLAM-ER Stand-off Land Attack Missile Expanded Response
SUU Suspended Underwing Unit

TALD Tactical Air-Launched Decoy
TIALD Thermal Imaging and Lazer Designation
TEMP Tornado Essential Modification Programme
TMD Tactical Munitions Dispenser
TOW Tube-launched Optically tracked, Wire-guided
TRIGAT *TRoisiéme* Generation Anti-Tank

UAV Unmanned Air Vehicle
USAF United States Air Force
USMC United States Marine Corps
USN United States Navy

WAFAR Wrap Around Fin Air Rocket
WCMD Wind-Corrected Munition Dispenser
WSO Weapons Systems Operator

The following lists detail the NATO and US DoD reporting codes for weapons used by the former Warsaw Pact. They are listed here for interest as they are still referred to and a small number are included on the inventory of member nations of NATO.

The use of the code systems listed here commenced in the early fifties and many are no longer in service. Their inclusion in these lists does not infer that they are currently in NATO inventory.

NATO code names for Russian built air to air missiles

R-1	AA-1 Alkali
R-2	AA-1 Alkali
R-3	AA-2 Atoll
R-4	AA-5 Ash
R-8	AA-3 Anab
R-9	AA-4 Awl
R-13	AA-2 Atoll
R-23	AA-7 Apex
R-24	AA-7 Apex
R-27	AA-10 Alamo
R-30	AA-3 Anab
R-33	AA-9 Amos
R-37	AA--9, AA-13
R-40	AA-6 Acrid
R-46	AA-6 Acrid
R-55	AA-1 Alkali
R-60	AA-8 Aphid
R-73	AA-11 Archer
R-74	AA-11 Archer
R-77	AA-12 Adder
R-98	AA-3 Anab
R-131	AA-2 Atoll

Russian air to air missiles from NATO codes

AA-1	Alkali	R-1, R-2, R-55
AA-2	Atoll	R-3, R-13, R-131
AA-3	Anab	R-8, R-30, R-98
AA-4	Awl	R-9
AA-5	Ash	R-4
AA-6	Acrid	R-40, R-46
AA-7	Apex	R-23, R-24
AA-8	Aphid	R-60
AA-9	Amos	R-33, R-37
AA-10	Alamo	R-27
AA-11	Archer	R-73, R-74
AA-12	Adder	R-77
AA-13	Arrow	R-37M

NATO code names for Russian built air to ground missiles

9M114	AS-8*
BL-10	AS-19 Koala
K-10	AS-2 Kipper
Kh-15	AS-16 Kickback
Kh-20	AS-3 Kangaroo
Kh-22 Burya	AS-4 Kitchen
Kh-23	AS-7 Kerry

Kh-25	AS-10 Karen	
Kh-25MP	AS-12 Kegler	
Kh-26	AS-6 Kingfish	
Kh-27	AS-12 Kegler	
Kh-28	AS-9 Kyle	
Kh-29	AS-14 Kedge	
Kh-31	AS-17 Krypton	
Kh-35	AS-20 Kayak	
Kh-37	AS-20 Kayak	
Kh-55	AS-15 Kent	
Kh-58	AS-11 Kitter	
Kh-59 Ovod	AS-13 Kingbolt	
Kh-59M Ovod M	AS-18 Kazoo	
Kh-65	AS-15 Kent	
Kh-66 Grom	AS-7 Kerry	
Kh-90	AS-19 Koala	
KR-1	AS-17 Krypton	
KS-1	AS-1 Kennel	
KSR-2	AS-5 Kelt	
KSR-5	AS-6 Kingfish	
KSR-11	AS-5 Kelt	
RKV-15	AS-16 Kickback	
RKV-500	AS-15 Kent	

*Reclassified as AT-8

NATO code names for Russian built air to ground missiles

AS-1	Kennel	KS-1
AS-2	Kipper	K-10
AS-3	Kangaroo	Kh-20
AS-4	Kitchen	Kh-22 Burya
AS-5	Kelt	KSR-2 / 11
AS-6	Kingfish	Kh-26, KSR-5
AS-7	Kerry	Kh-23 / Kh-66 Grom
AS-8		9M114 *
AS-9	Kyle	Kh-28
AS-10	Karen	Kh-25
AS-11	Kitter	Kh-58
AS-12	Kegler	Kh-25MP / Kh-27
AS-13	Kingbolt	Kh-59 Ovod
AS-14	Kedge	Kh-29
AS-15	Kent	Kh-55, RKV-500, Kh-65
AS-16	Kickback	Kh-15 / RKV-15
AS-17	Krypton	Kh-31 / KR-1
AS-18	Kazoo	Kh-59M Ovod M
AS-19	Koala	Kh-90 / BL-10
AS-20	Kayak	Kh-35 / Kh-37

NATO codes for Russian built anti-tank missiles

3M6 Shmel	AT-1 Snapper
9M14 Malyutka	AT-3 Sagger
9M17 Skorpion	AT-2 Swatter
9M112 Cobra	AT-8 Songster*
9M111 Faktoriya	AT-4 Spigot
9M114 Kokon	AT-6 Spiral
9M113 Konkurs	AT-5 Spandrel
9M114M1 / 2 Shturm 2 / 3	AT-9 Spiral 2

9M115 / 6 Metis	AT-13
9M117 Bastion	AT-10 Songster
9M119 Reflex	AT-11 Sniper
9M120 Vikhr / Ataka	AT-12 Swinger
9M120M Vikhr-M	AT-16
9M121 Vikhr-M	AT-16
9M123	AT-15
9M127	AT-15
9M131 Metis	AT-13
9M133 Kornet	AT-14

* Originally designated AS-8

Russian anti-tank missiles from NATO codes

AT-1	Snapper	3M6 Shmel
AT-2	Swatter	9M17 Skorpion
AT-3	Sagger	9M14 Malyutka
AT-4	Spigot	9M111 Faktoriya
AT-5	Spandrel*	9M113 Konkurs
AT-6	Spiral	9M114 Kokon
AT-7	Saxhorn	9M115 / 6 Metis
AT-8	Songster	9M112 Cobra
AT-9	Spiral 2	9M114M1 / 2 Shturm 2 / 3
AT-10	Songster	9M117 Bastion
AT-11	Sniper	9M119 Reflex
AT-12	Swinger	9M120 Vikhr / Ataka
AT-13		9M131 Metis
AT-14		9M133 Kornet
AT-15		9M123 / 7
AT-16		9M120M / 9M121 Vikhr-M

* Originally designated AS-8

OPPOSITE: A USAF McDonnell Douglas F-15E Strike Eagle of the 484th FS, 48th FW. This unit is based at RAF Lakenheath, Suffolk in the UK and assigned to NATO. It was photographed here over the Adriatic during NATO operations against Serb targets in the former Yugoslavia and armed with AIM-120 AMRAAM, AIM-9 Sidewinder missiles & LGB bombs.